Early Learning Standards and Staff Development

ALSO BY GAYE GRONLUND:

Focused Early Learning: A Planning Framework for Teaching Young Children

Focused Portfolios: A Complete Assessment for the Young Child (with Bev Engel)

Make Early Learning Standards Come Alive: Connecting Your Practice and Curriculum to State Guidelines

BY GAYE GRONLUND AND MARLYN JAMES:

Focused Observations: How to Observe Children for Assessment and Curriculum

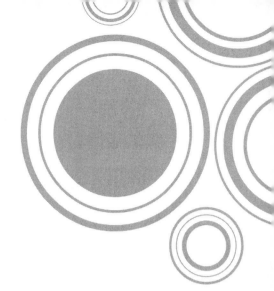

Early Learning Standards and Staff Development

Best Practices in the Face of Change

Gaye Gronlund *and* Marlyn James

 Redleaf Press®
www.redleafpress.org
800-423-8309

Published by Redleaf Press
10 Yorkton Court
St. Paul, MN 55117
www.redleafpress.org

First edition 2008
Cover design by Mayfly Design
Interior typeset in Whitman and designed by Mayfly Design
Interior photos by the authors
Printed in the United States of America
15 14 13 12 11 10 09 08   2 3 4 5 6 7 8 9

Library of Congress Cataloging-in-Publication Data
Gronlund, Gaye, 1952-
  Early learning standards and staff development : best practices in the face of change / Gaye Gronlund and Marlyn James. -- 1st ed.
     p. cm.
  Includes bibliographical references.
  ISBN 978-1-933653-31-0 (alk. paper)
  1. Early childhood education--Curricula--United States. 2. Early childhood education--Standards--United States. 3. Curriculum planning--United States. 4. Teachers--In-service training--United States. I. James, Marlyn. II. Title.
  LB1139.4.G75 2007
  372.19--dc22
                              2007022580

Printed on acid-free paper

FSC
Mixed Sources
Product group from well-managed
forests and other controlled sources

Cert no. SW-COC-002283
www.fsc.org
© 1996 Forest Stewardship Council

To Judy C.,
the depth of our friendship knows no bounds

—*GAYE*

*With love to my children, Patrick, Scott, and Kevin,
and to my grandchildren, Kyle, Ian, and Emilee*

—*MARLYN*

Early Learning Standards and Staff Development

Acknowledgments

The state leaders, monitors, mentors, and teachers involved in the New Mexico PreK Project

Suzi Boyett and the teachers of Project Reach Out in Lebanon and Western Boone Schools in Indiana

The Early Childhood Education Students at Flathead Valley Community College, Kalispell, Montana

The editorial staff at Redleaf Press

Our friend and colleague, Laila Aaen

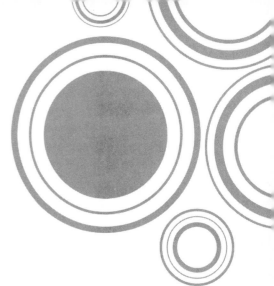

Introduction: Coping with the Changes in Early Childhood Education Today

As the twenty-first century has begun, early childhood education has undergone some major changes. These changes have wide-ranging effects on what is happening for young children in child care, preschool, and prekindergarten programs. The directors, staff development specialists, coaches, and mentors involved with these programs have been placed in a very difficult position. How do they effectively help their teaching staff to embrace the changes and yet not give up what they know are best practices for young children? These practices include play-based curricular approaches and authentic assessment methods. In this book, we will explore these issues and provide ideas and strategies for early childhood leaders to help them address these changes and to provide staff development and ongoing support to the teachers in their programs.

In our work as college instructors and consultants, we feel deeply committed to helping those in the field do what is best for young children. We also recognize that change can be a good thing. We think that as a field, we must grow and learn, and continue to develop in order to be relevant and viable. Yet we must remain true to our core beliefs and incorporate them into the change process. We believe that there are many good things happening in relation to early education today. We also have some serious concerns and hear those concerns voiced by directors, specialists, teachers, and care providers in our work with them. We recognize that the change process can be difficult and takes time. We hope this book will provide ways to embrace the changes going on in early education that are beneficial to children, and to resist and oppose those that are not in their best interests. This book is for those in leadership as staff development specialists and program directors who share our commitment and concerns.

The Changes in Early Education Today

What's in the mix then? What are the primary changes we see happening in early education? We see the following six changes as having an impact at this time:

1. The general public is seeing the benefits of early education.
2. Early learning standards have been developed by most U.S. states.
3. NAEYC has revised its accreditation requirements.
4. A clear definition of curriculum in early education has not been articulated, resulting in inappropriate and inadequate curricula often being recommended and adopted.
5. Calls for accountability have raised a debate about the best assessment approaches for young children.
6. Early educators have been resistant to change, unsure about the direction in which the above changes were taking the field.

We will elaborate on each of these changes.

Recognition of the Benefits of Early Education

First and foremost, the general public, politicians, and policymakers have recognized that there are benefits to early education. Hooray! This is good news. Many governors have started initiatives to support PreK programs or to fund all-day kindergarten. Long-term research studies, such as the Perry Preschool Project (Schweinhart et al. 2005) and the Carolina Abecedarian Project (Campbell et al. 2001), have received publicity in major newspapers and magazines. Their findings of long-term positive results of preschool interventions have helped fuel the political climate that has placed more emphasis on providing services to young children.

States Are Developing Learning Standards

This new valuing of preschool education has resulted in the development of learning standards for preschoolers in most states across the nation. This development is within a climate of emphasis on standards in kindergarten through twelfth grade as well. How those early learning standards are used and what impact they have on the practices of early educators may vary from state to state. They can become a helpful tool to identify common expectations across early childhood programs. But among early childhood professionals they have raised many fears and worries that are finding expression in an increasing number of workshops on this topic in conferences across the country. In session after session, discussions focus around how best to respond to the inappropriate uses of early learning standards and how to be more clear about what the field believes is right for young children. At the NAEYC Professional Development Conference in San Antonio in June of 2006 we heard questions such as:

- Will the recommended practices of planning for play and exploration go by the wayside? Will they be replaced by direct instruction focusing on skills found in the early learning standards?
- Will the individualization that has been so treasured by early educators be replaced by a one-size-fits-all approach to teaching and learning?
- Will authentic assessment be replaced by inappropriate testing or on-demand assessments tied to the early learning standards?

NAEYC Accreditation Requirements Revised

The National Association for the Education of Young Children (NAEYC) has recently revised its requirements for accreditation, including some new language regarding curriculum and assessment. To receive accreditation, a program is expected to have "a written statement of philosophy and use one or more written curricula or curriculum frameworks consistent with its philosophy that address central aspects of child development" (NAEYC 2006). The expectations around assessment endorse authentic assessment procedures but require that programs be ready to clarify their assessment processes. Many early educators welcome more meat and substance to the accreditation requirements so that an accredited program truly does reflect the best practices endorsed by the field. However, many are questioning just what the recommendations regarding curriculum and assessment mean. Must educators buy a published curricular package? If they have been using an assessment process designed in-house, will that meet the criteria for accreditation? Again, fears and worries are heard from the field.

Lack of a Clear Definition of Curriculum

With the early learning standards and the accreditation requirements, many early educators perceive that there is now a push for some sort of standardized curriculum for preschoolers. They wonder if they can justify activity times where children play and investigate with blocks, art materials, dramatic play materials, manipulatives, and sand and water. They fear that the push for meeting standards will require that they engage in more teacher-led group times with a focus on literacy and math skills, and less on providing opportunities for children to develop those skills as well as other concepts and knowledge as they play, participating in self-directed activities with adults as guides and facilitators.

Ultimately, we think the crux of the matter is the lack of the clear definition of curriculum that is just right for preschoolers. Early education is now functioning within a climate of external pressures from policymakers and the public. Both are demanding that learning and standards be the focus of preschool programs. Within that climate, then, early educators are struggling to define preschool curriculum. The criticism, "All they do is play in that program," still stings. Parents ask whether their child will experience enough academics to be ready for kindergarten and first grade. Policymakers ask for curricular approaches that clearly address the early learning standards developed for the state. Funding agencies expect a formal curriculum to be adopted, assuming that will mean that their money is well spent in supporting a particular program. Early educators who have long supported developmentally appropriate practices (DAP) are at a loss as to how to translate that set of philosophical beliefs into a coherent curricular framework. Publishers are stepping into this vacuum and providing packaged curricula that may address some aspects of the new requirements and expectations. However, some of these packaged curricula are woefully lacking in their adaptability, both to the unique needs of different settings, and to the individual needs of each child—two traits long recognized as vital to quality care and education. Instead of responding to the challenge by explaining how their teachers are addressing curriculum as they plan for children's play and interactions throughout each day, many early childhood leaders are succumbing to the pressures and purchasing inappropriate curricula just to be able to say to funding agencies and policymakers: "*This* is what we use."

Questions about Assessment

The increased accountability includes more attention to assessment practices. Again, the changing climate in kindergarten through twelfth grade education has been influential, meaning testing has become more and more prevalent. This has brought many outside of the field of early education to assume testing will be right for preschoolers as well. The field has responded with position papers and recommendations for authentic assessment methods such as teacher observation, portfolios, and checklists (NAEYC and NAECS/SDE 2003). But as calls for reliability and validity dominate the debate, driving the need for large-scale data collection and reporting, the recommended practices of observation and portfolios have been received by some as cumbersome and unscientific. Determining methods for gleaning numerical data from teachers' anecdotal records or portfolios is difficult and labor-intensive. Authentic assessment procedures are sometimes being thrown out for that reason alone, as the pressures to measure children's performance can appear overwhelming to many early educators.

Resistance to Change

Those of us involved in the field of early education are a special group of people. We often describe our jobs as joyful as we revel in the curiosity and enthusiasm of the children and relish their accomplishments. We feel we are giving much-needed services to families, and we enjoy the strong relationships that we build with parents and children. In this new climate of standards and accountability, the changes occurring—including the additional paperwork and reporting that are often required—may not appear to some teachers to be in the best interest of children. Therefore teachers may resist making changes. The results can vary, from low staff morale to teachers moving slowly in implementing new curricular and assessment practices, all the way to teachers deciding to leave the field completely.

Resistance to change is normal and healthy. In fact, it can become a part of the change process itself. However, when the changes are breaking the spirits of dedicated early childhood professionals and causing them to lose their passion and compromise their beliefs about what is best for young children, something is terribly wrong. We believe strongly that there are ways to embrace the good points about the changes going on in early education today and to redefine them in such a way as to eliminate the negative elements. As a field, we owe it to ourselves and to the children and families we serve to remain committed to our core beliefs and speak out boldly with a clearly articulated message. We want others to see the value of early education and the specific qualities that make it valuable for children, and to see that play-based curricular approaches can address learning standards and be assessed through authentic measures.

The Focus of This Book

In this book, we will explore in depth the issue of early learning standards and how they can be integrated into curriculum and assessment practices that are just right for young children. Suggestions for planning and implementing effective staff development sessions will be shared. Ideas for providing coaching and ongoing support to teachers, as well as dealing with resistance to change, will be offered. We will provide frameworks and tools that will help early educators represent to others the ways in which early education is most beneficial to children. We will address change issues and provide suggestions for dealing with change effectively. And we will provide numerous ideas and strategies for the leaders in the field of early childhood education to help their teaching staffs grow and learn. We hope this book will empower each reader to figure out the best ways to help others adapt to the many changes in early education today and to continue to work on behalf of children each and every day.

Chapter 1 will address the misperception that there is no connection between developmentally appropriate practices and early learning standards. Chapter 2 will focus on the change process and offer management techniques and ideas to help early childhood leaders effectively deal with the changes in the field. In chapter 3 we will share our philosophy regarding staff development strategies. Chapters 4 through 7 will focus on twenty-four staff development activities to help teachers integrate early learning standards and best practices in curriculum and authentic assessment. In chapter 8, we will provide additional coaching and mentoring strategies to help teachers make changes in their practices for both curriculum and assessment.

We want early education teachers, directors, and administrators to no longer feel defensive or inadequate in responding to inappropriate expectations from policymakers and funding agencies. Rather, we want early childhood professionals to gather together in a beautiful chorus of voices to tell others what we know and believe are the best ways to provide quality education to young children in the U.S. We believe that staff development specialists, program directors, mentors, and coaches have the important task of conducting this chorus of voices! We hope that this book will provide you with many ideas, tips, and strategies to help as you work in your leadership role with teachers, assisting them in embracing the good things in the changes in early education today and resisting the inappropriate things.

References

Campbell, F. A., E. P. Pungello, S. Miller-Johnson, M. Burchinal, and C. T. Ramey. 2001. The development of cognitive and academic abilities: Growth curves from an early childhood educational experiment. *Developmental Psychology* 37:231–242.

Lynch, Robert G. 2006. Preschool pays. In *Annual editions: Early childhood education 06/07,* 27th ed., ed. Karen Menke Paciorek. Dubuque, Iowa: McGraw Hill Contemporary Learning Series.

National Association for the Education of Young Children. 2006. NAEYC Academy for early childhood program accreditation. Accessed June 5, 2007, at www.naeyc.org/academy/standards.

National Association for the Education of Young Children and the National Association of Early Childhood Specialists in State Departments of Education (NAECS/SDE). 2003. Where we stand on curriculum, assessment, and program evaluation. Accessed June 5, 2007, at www.naeyc.org/about/positions/cape.asp.

Schweinhart, L. J., J. Montie, Z. Xiang, W. S. Barnett, C. R. Belfield, and M. Nores. 2005. *Lifetime effects: The High/Scope perry preschool study through age 40.* Ypsilanti, Mich.: High/Scope Press.

Addressing the Disconnect: Early Learning Standards and Developmentally Appropriate Practice Do Go Together!

From our experiences in talking with early educators across the country, we hear a common theme being expressed: a genuine distrust that early learning standards and developmentally appropriate practices can coexist in quality early childhood programs. We believe that standards have the potential to be an important part of our commitment to quality education for young children. They can be used to enhance planning and curriculum and to insure that all children have opportunities to maximize their developmental potential. We are also keenly aware of the potential for misuse of these standards. We advocate that all early childhood professionals must be ready to take a stand against inappropriate uses of early learning standards, to continually ask questions and raise concerns so that standards are used to the benefit of young children.

We see several misunderstandings regarding standards in the field of early education. In this chapter we will identify these misunderstandings and offer facts and suggestions for helping others understand the possibilities of incorporating standards more fully in developmentally appropriate ways. We will address:

- the difference between explicit and implicit standards
- the misunderstanding that the expectations in early learning standards are not age-appropriate
- the mistaken assumption that every child of a certain age will be expected to accomplish every standard for that age
- the mistaken notion that incorporating early learning standards necessarily means direct teaching in teacher-led activities only

- the misunderstanding that the kind of learning required to meet standards can't take place in the natural course of play
- the assumption that assessing for early learning standards means testing or on-demand assessments only
- the conclusion that early childhood educators will have to set aside their passion for supporting children's development across all learning domains in order to address the standards, for example, focusing on literacy and math skills to the detriment of social and emotional development

Explicit and Implicit Standards

We believe that there is no one right way to embrace standards in curriculum and assessment practices. The unique needs of individual children and the variations in group dynamics within different constellations of children will come into play, as will the unique characteristics of families and communities. How teachers incorporate early learning standards differs depending on several factors, including the:

- overall developmental level of a particular group
- unique experiences each child brings to the group
- variations in group dynamics caused by children's individual differences
- cultural influences of different families and communities
- experiences of the teachers involved

Keeping these factors in mind allows each teacher to look differently at the ways in which the early learning standards will come alive in her classroom.

We often see distrust expressed by early educators in regard to implementing standards. We think this distrust is based to a large extent on the common misunderstandings that we identified earlier. The irony of the matter is that early educators almost always have goals and expectations for the children they work with—which is really just another way of talking about standards. Whether spoken or unspoken, all adults working with young children have ideas about what the children should be doing and what is important for them to be learning. Barbara Bowman (2006, 43) states: "But, it is not true that programs that say they have no standards actually have no standards. What it means is that standards are implicit, imbedded in the particular biases of a teacher, parent, or whatever other adults are making decisions. When a program has no standards it really means that everyone gets to use their own standards without subjecting them to scrutiny. . . . The result here is that it is difficult to determine what teachers are teaching and children are learning."

Bowman also advocates informed consent: "Informed consent demands that teachers and programs advertise and be accountable for the education they offer children and what they expect them to learn. . . . Since young children cannot give informed consent, parents and the community must." We see this as a call for accountability: being explicit about goals and expectations for children so that parents, teachers, community members, and policy makers have a clear idea of what they are.

The Age Appropriateness of State Standards

Contrary to the perception of many educators, the early learning standards that have been developed across the country *are* age-appropriate because, in each state, they were written and reviewed by early childhood professionals familiar with the developmental needs of young children. We have each been a part of the standards development process in different states. In our experiences, the professionals involved paid very close attention to being age-appropriate and developmentally sensitive. And in her review of national standards for her book *Make Early Learning Standards Come Alive*, Gaye Gronlund found strong similarities from state to state, and similar expectations based on sound developmental knowledge. The following are examples from our work with standards development.

In the State of Montana, time and attention were given to insure that the process for developing the Montana Early Learning Guidelines was inclusive of the state's diverse early childhood community. In the beginning stages, six early childhood professionals developed a steering committee to consider the issues involved in creating developmentally appropriate early learning guidelines, including who should be a part of the process of developing the standards. The committee researched the standards of other states and then invited about sixty people to participate in the creation of a rough draft of early learning guidelines. The group consisted of interested early childhood education stakeholders in the state including, but not limited to, family child care providers, center teachers and directors, health care professionals, therapists, college professors, representatives of the Montana Early Childhood Services Bureau, and representatives from the Montana Office of Public Instruction.

The work of the large group was to develop the specific criteria for each content area. Before coming together, participants submitted a list of interest areas and then worked in small groups to develop the specifics of each guideline that was to be included. After the rough draft was edited for consistency, it was sent out to interested parties in the state for comments and review. After a review time of about six months, the guidelines were published and available to anyone who was interested. A family-friendly version is also available.

In the State of New Mexico, the development of prekindergarten learning outcomes and essential indicators took place over a three-year process. Early educators from around the state were invited to participate in a series of focus groups and working sessions to contribute their knowledge and to provide feedback on several draft versions. Special attention was paid to the diversity of the state's unique population mix, and meetings included participants from various cultural groups so that attention was paid to their particular needs. An initial set of outcomes was published and used in the first year of state-funded prekindergarten programs. Teacher feedback was then gathered at the first prekindergarten institute to be used in edits and revisions of the outcomes so that they were not only developmentally appropriate, but also teacher-friendly and tied to specific observational assessment tools. Again, this process involved input from early educators and cultural representatives around the state. In addition, attention was paid to the work from other states around the country so that the revised outcomes incorporated the best possible thinking of not only New Mexicans but also other early childhood professionals nationally.

Children's Accomplishment of Standards

Few early childhood educators would expect each child to accomplish every learning standard for his or her age group. Most of us agree that the job of early education is to build foundational skills and that standards are intended to be a guideline for tracking a child's progress in gaining these skills. Each child will demonstrate progress along a continuum that reflects strengths and weaknesses relative to an established norm, while taking individual characteristics into account. Looking at each child's progress toward achieving standards at her own pace keeps early educators focused on goals and expectations and allows for each child's individuality to shine through at the same time. For example, in the content area of literacy, no early educator should expect to have to teach four-year-olds how to read paragraphs. We do expect to help four-year-olds to develop the skills and understanding needed to appreciate and enjoy books, to begin to recognize their names and some alphabet letters, and to recognize that print has meaning, for example, that it represents the words we speak and that words can be written down. The same principle applies to other content areas such as math and science. The reality is that early educators do need to be accountable for documenting each child's progress *toward* achieving each standard.

Curriculum and Standards

We believe that offering a wide variety of rich experiences designed to meet the needs of each child *and* to be developmentally appropriate for the group supports children's movement along a continuum of standards-based learning. In this way, early learning standards can be addressed through traditional early childhood teaching strategies, which include:

- play and exploration in a carefully planned environment with teachers as facilitators and guides
- teachers making the most of learning in daily routines such as snack, outdoor exploration, toileting and hand washing, and arrival and departure
- teacher-led small and large group times

"Planning curriculum with early learning standards in mind does not require a complete change in teaching practices. . . . [It] requires adding a layer of awareness to your planning and implementation so that you can clearly see where standards are being addressed and add ways to bring them more to the forefront" (Gronlund 2006, 16). We strongly believe that standards can be incorporated into programs without giving up the most enjoyable parts about working with young children, such as spontaneity, discovering each child's emerging skills and interests, and the opportunity to develop our own unique skills and interests. Staff development and ongoing mentoring and support are necessary to help teachers learn to integrate standards into their existing curricular practices. The scope of the curriculum can continue to be broad and comprehensive, incorporating all of the developmental domains.

Play and Learning

Early childhood developmental theory has long informed us that play is the way that children learn best (Stegelin 2005). Teachers make play and learning come together through thoughtful planning and reflection. The challenge becomes one of recognizing when children's play offers opportunities for learning within the domains covered by state standards. These learning opportunities can be developed through children's spontaneous play themes and can then be related to specific standards. Early educators can plan for play episodes with specific standards in mind and then observe and document how the children use the play to move along the standards continuum. "The teacher becomes a true artist as he or she weaves the many social, emotional, intellectual, physical and cultural opportunities children bring to the classroom" (Oliver and Klugman 2006, 13–14).

Assessment and Standards

We have talked about how, contrary to some common misperceptions, early educators can use authentic assessment methods—observational assessment and portfolios, for example—to document children's progress toward the standards. Such assessment can guide instruction, helping teachers to be better at reaching each child where she is performing, and helping her to move on in her development. In this age of accountability, however, assessments may also be used to determine "whether [the child's] knowledge is what the program said it taught. Accountability assessments are, of course, the most problematic since they hold teachers, administrators, and educational systems accountable for what children have learned" (Bowman 2006, 48). A part of the confusion in some programs is that the two kinds of assessment are going on at the same time. The early educators are documenting observations and gathering work samples in a portfolio to be given to families, and the program administrators are "testing" the children to assess their progress in differing developmental domains, with no connection between the two. We believe that the inappropriateness of such assessment strategies should be challenged. Staff development sessions focusing on observational techniques and careful documentation of children's learning are a necessary part of making this happen.

Early Educators' Passion and Standards

Early educators can keep their passion alive as they embrace standards if they integrate them into practices that they know in their hearts and minds are just right for young children. They are in danger of losing that passion when they succumb to inappropriate pressures and do not fight back as advocates for best practices for children. This takes energy, enthusiasm, knowledge, and, most important, courage. Effective leaders can be a very important part of empowering teachers. Through staff development, coaching, and mentoring, program directors, mentors, and staff development specialists can help teachers work together to recognize the beneficial changes that standards and accountability can bring to programs and to continually work to correct the detrimental changes.

It takes time for early educators to learn, grow, and feel comfortable with this process of change and to make standards come alive in curriculum and assessment. In the next chapter, we will discuss the change process and provide techniques and ideas for managing effective change.

References

Bowman, Barbara T. 2006. Standards at the heart of educational equity. *Young Children* 61(5):42–48.

Gronlund, Gaye. 2006. *Make early learning standards come alive: Connecting your practice and curriculum to state guidelines.* St. Paul: Redleaf Press.

Montana's early learning guidelines. Accessed June 13, 2007, at www .montana.edu/ecp/pdfs/MTEarlyLearningGuidelines.pdf.

New Mexico early learning outcomes. Accessed June 1, 2007, at www .newmexicoprek.org/index.cfm?event=public.prek.Materials.

Oliver, Susan J., and Edgar Klugman. 2006. Play and standards-driven curricula: Can they work together in preschool? *Child Care Exchange* (July/ August 2006)12–16.

Stegelin, Dolores A. 2005. Making the case for play policy: Research-based reasons to support play-based environments. *Young Children* 60(2):76–85.

The Change Process

Change is difficult for everyone. Change, by definition, implies having to deal with something that's unfamiliar, which can seem frightening at times. Change can threaten our comfort zone and put us into a state of disequilibrium. Yet change is a constant factor in life. As standards and greater accountability become more and more accepted as part of early education, we are finding that we have no choice but to develop strategies to deal with what these changes may mean for our programs. In this chapter we will explore the change process, share resources that we, as college instructors and consultants, have found helpful, and talk about our experiences with the following aspects of change:

- the fact that change is inevitable
- the emotional aspects of change
- the naturalness of resistance to change and ways to work with different forms of resistance
- ways to manage the change process.

We have learned that the change process is occurring on two levels. Staff development specialists and program directors are in leadership roles as "change champions." They are leading the charge in helping teachers integrate early learning standards and embrace accountability. Yet, we have found that these change champions also have feelings about the changes going on in the field. They may be functioning outside of their own comfort zone at times, as well as dealing with the reactions of the teachers with whom they work. And on top of all that, they must also maintain their passion and commitment to what's best for young children and make sure that they and their teachers stay true to what is known about how children learn. That's a tall order!

The Inevitability of Change

We recognize that managing the change process is not an easy task. Yet we feel strongly that it is a necessary one that program leaders must take on. The more attention and consideration we give it, the easier it will be to facilitate the process of change for both ourselves and the teachers with whom we work.

One easy but important way to start is to give voice to people's natural concerns about change. The following sayings from folk wisdom (Harvey 1995) do just that. Look over this list. Do any of these sayings resonate with you more than others? You can ask teachers if they identify with any of them as well.

> *Stress is fertile ground for success.*
> *If you want change, have a party.*
> *Change is loss.*
> *You learn to walk only by taking baby steps.*
> *Change is in the mind of the participants, not in the organization.*
> *Change without growth fades away.*
> *Change is inevitable; pain is optional.*
> *Change is inevitable; growth is optional.*

Change is indeed inevitable. In our experiences, we have seen that most of the problems that arise in an organization facing change are because of individuals' negative reactions to that change. And in general, those reactions are emotional in nature. As one of the sayings above states, change is often perceived as loss—a loss of the familiar, of "the way we've always done things." When faced with such a loss, many of us cling even tighter to our old ways and ideas and resist letting go. If forced to change, we may react the way someone grieving a loss would: we get angry and may act out either subtly or overtly. Besides, we may feel that we already have too much to do and don't have any more energy to give to making changes that we don't necessarily understand or agree with.

This is especially true in early childhood education, where wages and working conditions are not always supportive of the additional professional expertise and new knowledge that seem to be demanded by the inclusion of standards in curriculum and assessment.

> *Someone once described going into the 21st century as akin to living in permanent white water. Child care teachers know this feeling well and, depending on their disposition, put their energies into damming the waters, ferociously paddling to keep up, or actively scanning for the optimal balance between challenge and safety. Helping teachers cultivate*

a disposition to expect continuous change and challenge enhances their responsiveness to classroom dynamics and sustains their ability to ride out the continual demands and frustrations of their job.

In the above quote, Elizabeth Jones (1994, x) describes a process that many of us must go through in order to recover from the loss we perceive as changes are introduced. We must recognize and name what we feel we have lost. We may need to rant and rave in anger and denial until we accept that the change is inevitable and necessary. Then and only then can we embrace it and truly grow in our thinking and our practice. And that process takes time and effort.

The Emotional Components of Change

We have all had experiences with change processes that have failed. James Flaherty identifies some of the reasons for this in what he refers to as the "Amoeba Theory." In it he describes why some change efforts, no matter how well intended, ultimately fail. He informs us that amoeba change their behavior by being given a poke or some sugar. Similarly, "managers and coaches attempt to bring about changes in others by figuring out how to poke them or give them sugar" (Flaherty 1999, 7). However, Flaherty states, while this works well for the amoeba, ultimately people resent being manipulated. Leaders may provide incentives or make threats, and they might see teachers change their behavior at first. But as soon as the reward or threat ends, so does the new behavior. These short-term reward and punishment approaches limit the focus to the immediate consequences and they usually fail to achieve compliance over the long haul. These methods don't allow for individual creativity and curiosity, for making the changes one's own. People are more complex than laboratory animals responding only to extrinsic threats or rewards. We need to be an active part of the change process, not a passive recipient.

Michael Fullan (1993, 40) identifies lessons of what he calls "dynamic change" that involve multiple aspects of human behavior:

There is a pattern underlying the eight lessons of dynamic change and it concerns one's ability to work with polar opposites: simultaneously pushing for change while allowing self-learning to unfold; being prepared for a journey of uncertainty; seeing problems as sources of creative resolution; having a vision, but not being blinded by it; valuing the individual and the group; incorporating centralizing and decentralizing forces; being internally cohesive, but externally oriented; and valuing, personal change . . . as the route to system change.

In the following story, Marlyn James describes her own "journey of uncertainty" as a director of an early childhood program, as well as those of her staff.

> *Years ago I began directing a new program. I came with a great deal of administrative experience and education in early childhood. I thought that the program was very similar to the one that I had left and assumed that the teaching staff and the families shared the same thoughts, goals, and attitudes that I had regarding developmentally appropriate experiences for the children. I believe that they did in theory, but I was much too quick to try and implement changes that I thought were appropriate.*
>
> *I led discussions regarding the changes that I wanted to implement with the teachers. They would nod their heads and appear to agree with me. I thought that everything was fine until I began to realize that the teachers were going back to their old ways when they thought I wasn't watching. This really was a shock and a surprise to me. It took me a long time to understand why this was happening until I realized that change is a slow process. I learned that people need time to try new ideas in ways that work for them. Teachers need time to try new things without the worries of doing something "wrong." I also realized that the reality was that the program was very different from what I thought was appropriate for children and families. I came to understand that we had to come to a place in the middle of the road and that my trying to change things so quickly made the teachers feel like what they had been doing was wrong.*
>
> *So we began to talk about what things they would like to keep the same and what things they would be willing to change. The teachers began to implement some of my new ideas in the curriculum and in their daily interactions with children. Over time the program did change. And most importantly, the teachers and the families liked the changes that were happening. The lesson for me was that change is a slow and thoughtful process. It takes much more time than you wish, but the results are worth the wait!*

We agree that paying attention to the individual staff member's personal learning needs and styles, while recognizing and responding to the natural uncertainty in the process, can help you develop effective strategies as you plan for staff development sessions, introduce new directions, and attempt to lead teachers to embrace the changes.

In the case of early learning standards, we have found that one of the major losses that teachers fear in regard to making changes is the perceived loss of freedom. Many early educators have long planned their curriculum around children's interests and abilities as well as their own. Rather than being tied to "cookbook curricula," they've had the flexibility to set up a learning environment with a number of play possibilities for the children and then to "go with the flow," following the child's lead. For many who have been in the field for a long time, the emphasis has been on social/emotional development as a necessary foundation for academic learning. In their work with children, teachers focused on helping them learn to get along with each other, take turns, be kind, and manage their emotions and develop independence. Along the way, they also read books to encourage literacy, helped children write their names, counted everything in sight, and taught children about many aspects of their world. They knew that the academic learning was taking place, but they didn't feel quite as accountable for how that was happening, as is being demanded of them today.

Many of these early educators who have embraced emergent curriculum and play-based practices assume that in order to incorporate standards into curriculum and assessment practices for young children they must give up some of the most important aspects of sound teaching. They may assume that the only way to address standards is through direct instruction or teacher-led activities. It is your job as a "champion of change" to remind teachers that incorporating standards doesn't necessarily mean compromising their values or their understanding of best practices. The process of helping them embrace change will involve working through their resistance and helping them see that they can grow and evolve by learning to incorporate standards as they "go with the flow" and follow the children's lead in learning through play. In chapters 4 through 8, we will explore the issues of standards as they relate directly to curriculum planning and assessment more fully and will offer many ideas for staff development activities as well as for coaching and mentoring strategies.

The Healthiness of Resistance to Change

We have learned that it can actually be a good sign when adults resist change: "Defenses and resistance are a sign that you have touched something important and valuable" (Block 2000). As early educators push back or question the value of standards, they may be simply saying, "Oh dear. This is going to be different, but will it be better? I can see there might be some value here, but it's frightening to me to think how I might have to leave the comfort of the way I have always taught." As change champions, we have learned that this is much more encouraging than if changes are greeted with total apathy, with an attitude of "Who cares?" Apathy signals that there is little investment in what they've been doing and no concern about what value there may be in the changes. Resistance can show that the ideas have struck a chord and are being taken seriously (whether the person likes them or not). "[R]emember this: fear, anger, and complacency. These emotions are what stops change in its tracks" (Hight 2005).

It's hard not to take resistance personally. If you are a director or staff development specialist who is trying to help others learn more about your state's early learning standards and implement them in your program, you may feel that you, as the messenger, are being attacked, rather than the message you are attempting to deliver. "The main thing to do in coping successfully with resistance is to not take it personally . . . Resistant [staff] are defending against the fact that they are going to have to make a difficult choice, take an unpopular action, confront some reality that they have been trying to emotionally avoid" (Block 2000, 148).

Ways to Manage the Change Process

Figuring out why a teacher shows strong resistance to change can help you plan more effective strategies. Susan Harper-Whalen (2006, 1) identifies the following barriers that may affect individual practitioner's ability to change. They include:

- the power of past experiences in childhood and as a parent
- the impact of experience as an early childhood practitioner
- the role of self-esteem and the esteem of the early childhood field
- the challenge of translating early childhood theory into day-to-day practices with young children

We want to reemphasize our belief that allowing teachers to express their feelings, fears, and concerns about implementing standards in curriculum and assessment is a fundamental and necessary step in the process of moving them toward acceptance and growth. Creating a safe environment where they can share their own childhood experiences and talk about the difficulties in being an early educator helps them work through their resistance. We often lead brainstorming sessions where teachers share benefits and concerns as they begin working with standards. A little further on in the implementation, we start all meetings with what they see as their successes and challenges. Then we celebrate the successes and address the challenges.

Individualized learning is as important for adults as it is for children. Each person in your group will have different skills, knowledge, and learning styles, and will be at different points on the continuum from resistance to acceptance of new ideas. Those further along may have practical suggestions for those who are struggling. By putting the challenges on the table and identifying barriers and solutions, you all can move along in the change process together. The steps can be baby steps for some, leaps for others. Your role as the champion of the change process is to challenge teachers to embrace standards and use them in curriculum and assessment while recognizing each teacher as an individual and celebrating their small steps as well as their leaps forward.

In chapter 8, we will look at ways that resistance may be evident in curriculum and assessment practices in the classroom. We will give examples and strategies for working directly with teachers as a coach and mentor, to help them work through the change process and find their own ways of implementing new thinking within their comfort zone.

The Managing Complex Change Continuum

The continuum shown in the following graphic is very helpful in looking at the forms that resistance is taking. By looking at the reactions to change efforts, you can track back to the kinds of support that teachers need in order to continue to move forward toward the identified learning goal. Look at the top row of the graphic. There are five identified elements necessary for effective change to occur: Vision, Skills, Incentives, Resources, and Action Plan. As you look down each row, you can see that one of those elements is missing.

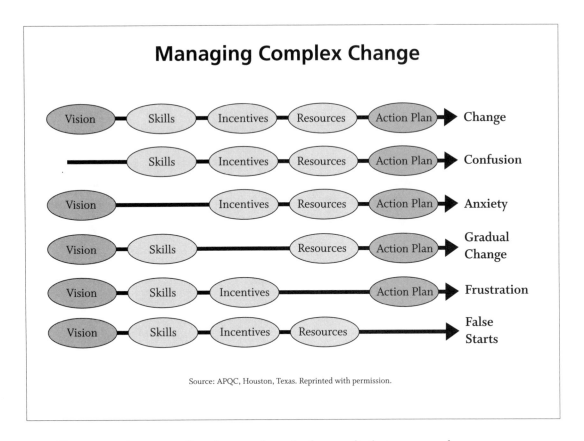

Managing Complex Change

| Vision | Skills | Incentives | Resources | Action Plan | → Change |

| | Skills | Incentives | Resources | Action Plan | → Confusion |

| Vision | | Incentives | Resources | Action Plan | → Anxiety |

| Vision | Skills | | Resources | Action Plan | → Gradual Change |

| Vision | Skills | Incentives | | Action Plan | → Frustration |

| Vision | Skills | Incentives | Resources | | → False Starts |

Source: APQC, Houston, Texas. Reprinted with permission.

The interesting part of each row, then, is the result that occurs when that element is missing. Let's go through each one and consider how it might be evidenced in regard to the changes resulting from implementing early learning standards, and greater accountability in curriculum and assessment in early childhood programs.

Confusion

If teachers are feeling confused, the vision may not be clear. They may say, "Okay. We know that we are supposed to implement these early learning standards. But what exactly does that mean?" We think teachers will find that revisiting the overarching goal of implementation and defining clearly the benefits of early learning standards may be all that is needed to move forward.

Anxiety

If anxiety is evident, it's likely that teachers fear that they are lacking the necessary skills to meet new expectations. In our experience, teachers who have long paid attention to social/emotional development as primary in the early childhood years may be uncertain as to just how to incorporate literacy, math, and science activities that are age-appropriate. Their only model may be the elementary classrooms in which they did their student teaching. They may have a gut instinct that the practices they saw there were not the best for younger children, but they do not have the skills to modify them in ways that are right for preschoolers. Some early educators may not even clearly define what they do as "teaching" and may think that they need to spend much more time in direct instruction in order to address early learning standards. These teachers may not yet understand that it's possible—much less know how—to incorporate the standards in playful exploration and investigation or in daily classroom routines.

Gradual Change

If change is too gradual, this probably is a result of lack of incentives. If you recognize that the change is happening at a pace that you feel is too slow (be careful not to expect too much, too soon!), teachers may need more incentives to embrace the change. We hear from teachers again and again that learning the standards themselves is a lot of work, let alone incorporating them in lesson and activity plans and assessing them authentically. How can you help your teachers to see the benefits of this work? Can you provide incentives related directly to their increasing professionalism? Can you reward them with planning time while you, as the director, take over their classroom? Can you leave them notes in their mailboxes letting them know what a great job they are doing? Can you encourage parents to let them know how much they are appreciated? Alerting your board of directors to new requirements for teachers and asking them for their support may be a way to obtain incentives that are meaningful to teachers. Can you do anything about wages or benefits that would reflect their growing skills and expanding efforts on behalf of children?

Frustration

A common cause for teachers' frustration with the change process is perceiving that the resources for implementing that change are insufficient or not even present. Teachers need resources to feel supported and do the job right. Opportunities to attend trainings and workshops related to implementation of standards are resources that will give them ideas and support from others. We find that most teachers identify time as a critical resource of which there is not enough. Release time once a week specifically designed for use in planning with standards in mind, or for collecting documentation and assessment information regarding the children's progress toward the standards, will be greatly appreciated. We do not want to set teachers up to fail. And unfortunately, many may feel that way as they see more and more requirements of accountability placed upon them and fewer and fewer resources provided to assist them in meeting those requirements. We have even heard of programs that monitor the amount of paper teachers use as they copy and fill out checklists tied to standards. This only adds to resistance and undermines success.

False Starts

You may see a little change here, a little change there—but then folks begin to return to their old ways. False starts result when there was no clearly defined action plan to follow. We often set a timeline with teachers for certain implementation goals such as: "By the end of this month, everyone will have written goals on their lesson plans tied to the standards." Then we address that part of the action plan at a staff meeting and let teachers express their successes and challenges with that process. In that way they learn from each other's experiences. For the next month, we schedule observation visits to see those written lesson goals in action. As the observer, we write down factual anecdotes about the questions and comments we hear teachers using as they engage children in conversation and support their learning as they play. We converse with individual teachers or with teaching teams to give them feedback regarding our observations, and continue setting target goals for curricular and assessment strategies. You can define ways that the group will address those goals throughout the year and make sure that your action plan has clear points and dates for both implementation and evaluation. The group may determine those, or there may be some that are identified by you. You can determine that based on your management style and your knowledge of your colleagues.

Celebrate Change

We strongly recommend that you plan some times for celebration as well! One of the folk sayings at the beginning of this chapter reads: "If you want change, have a party." Don't forget to provide the incentive of celebrating success (or even just hard work). Some groups have a funeral for the old ideas and a party for the new ones. Symbolism and rituals can be powerful! We encourage you to use them to your advantage as you continue to be a change champion in your work.

Being aware of how adults learn in meaningful and long-lasting ways is an important part of this process of change. In the next chapter, we will share our ideas and experiences regarding adult learning. We will talk about the importance of creating safe and trusting learning environments in which adults can take risks and learn and grow together.

References

Block, Peter. 2000. *Flawless consulting: A guide to getting your expertise used.* 2nd ed. San Diego: Pfeiffer & Company.

Flaherty, James. 1999. *Coaching: Evoking excellence in others.* Burlington, Mass.: Butterworth-Heinemann.

Fullan, Michael. 1993. *Change forces: Probing the depths of educational reform.* Levittown, Pa.: The Falmer Press.

Harper-Whalen, Susan. 2006. Potential barriers to change: Training solutions. *Montana Early Childhood Project* 12.

Harvey, Thomas R. 1995. *Checklist for change: A pragmatic approach to creating and controlling change.* Lancaster, Pa.: Technomic Publishing Co., Inc.

Hight, Gayle. 2005. Emotion is key to change, says Deloitte consulting principal. Accessed July 21, 2007, at www.mccombs.utexas.edu/news/pressreleases/cohen_10_05_wrap.asp.

Jones, Elizabeth. 1994. Foreword to *Training teachers: A harvest of theory and practice,* by Deb Curtis and Margie Carter. St. Paul: Redleaf Press.

Adult Learning and Quality Staff Development

We see creating effective learning opportunities for teachers as a two-pronged approach: planning and implementing staff development sessions followed by ongoing mentoring and coaching in the classroom. Staff development sessions will be more meaningful if they are interactive, playful, and full of exploration, with plenty of opportunities for the participants to share their concerns and reflect on the information provided. We agree with Margie Carter and Deb Curtis (1994, 7) when they say: "The bulk of any class or workshop we offer is spent in small group activities with choices for participation and opportunities to pursue their interests and learning styles."

You may notice that we do not use the word "training" in this book. In our opinion, "training" implies too much of a hierarchical relationship with an expert imparting knowledge to nonexperts. We think that a new paradigm for staff development is necessary: one where participants are on equal footing with staff development specialists who serve as mentors and coaches. We strive to create learning experiences where individuality and diversity are respected and embraced. Our experience as graduate students and as instructors at Pacific Oaks College has strongly influenced our thinking about these issues. We are grateful to our professors and mentors for the experiences and guidance they gave to us. In our work as consultants and college instructors, we have taken many of their recommendations to heart and employed active learning for adults. The ideas we share in this chapter reflect our studies as well as our experiences as staff development leaders.

We all want our mentoring and coaching efforts to result in positive changes in practice for the participants. If we want these efforts to be long lasting, we need to plan staff development opportunities that are relevant and meaningful to the participants. Our philosophy is based on the following principles of effective adult learning. We will address each one more fully in this chapter.

- Adult learners need to become emotionally connected.
- Adults need a safe environment for growth and learning in which they feel comfortable taking risks.
- Adults need to keep their passion for working with young children.
- Adults want to play too! They play with ideas and with other people.
- Adults need a meaningful framework for what they're learning. Therefore, for early childhood staff development session topics to be most meaningful and relevant, they should be presented in the context of a model for working with children that demonstrates developmentally appropriate practices.
- Adults have many different learning styles and experiences as teachers.
- Adults benefit most from ongoing learning opportunities, not one-shot workshops. Therefore, staff development sessions are most effective in combination with classroom coaching and mentoring that provide participants with opportunities to try things out.
- Adults need time for reflection in both staff development and coaching sessions.

In this time of change in the field of early childhood education, and with the calls for greater accountability and attention to standards, we believe even more strongly that staff development efforts need to embrace these principles. By combining them with the information about dealing with change from chapter 2, we hope you will find support for your role as a staff development leader. Then, in chapters 4 through 8, we will give you specific activity ideas for staff development sessions, and guidelines for coaching and mentoring staff around the changes relating to curriculum and assessment.

We are not going to give you set agendas for using the staff development activities in this book. Instead, we encourage you to read through all of the activities and determine which ones best fit your staff development situations. If you are a program director using periodic one-hour meetings as times to bring new information and ideas to your staff, you will want to choose the activities that best meet your goals. If you are a staff development specialist planning for full- or half-day sessions, you will want to incorporate more of the activities. You can choose those that address the topics that meet your goals.

Emotionally Connecting with Participants

As we plan for staff development opportunities we think about how the ideas or information will impact the participants on an emotional level. This requires a conscious effort at finding out who the participants are as people. What are their life experiences, ideas, and passions? It also means taking the time to articulate their issues of working daily in an early childhood education environment in general, and what their specific issues and concerns are regarding the topics at hand. We want the participants to be personally—which means emotionally—connected to the process of implementing new ideas and practices.

In staff development sessions, we usually begin with introductions and plans for the day. Then, very early in the agenda, we ask the participants questions such as:

- Can you tell us something about your work with children?
- What are your goals for today?
- What are your concerns regarding today's topic?
- Is there anything else that you want us to know before we begin?

Questions like these set the tone for the day and also give a clear message that we care about their issues and concerns and will try to find ways to meet their needs and answer their questions.

Throughout our sessions, we invite questions and comments from the participants. This can be a tricky business, however. We want to value each person's concerns, but we have all been in situations where one or two persons have dominated a discussion with questions not always related to the topic. We have found that creating a "parking lot," a physical space where you put such questions, communicates that you value all questions and still keeps everyone on topic. To make a parking lot, post a flipchart sheet labeled "Questions" and give participants sticky notes so that they can write down questions that come up that aren't directly related to the topic at hand and that can be put on hold until later. Be sure to let the group know when you will address those questions. In our work we sometimes deal with each question individually at a break or during a small group activity with the person who posed the question. We may also periodically look at the questions and answer them in the whole group. And, at times, we table a question completely and put it on the agenda for a future meeting because more information is needed to address it or different resources are necessary. The important point here is that you communicate a clear message that you are open, you are listening, and that you value particapants' concerns.

Establishing a Safe Environment for Growth and Learning

Letting participants know that you care about who they are and what they feel will help you develop a climate of safety and trust. Such an environment enables people to take risks. Just like children, adults need a sense of safety in order to learn, grow, and change. Abraham Maslow (1970) states that we function within a hierarchy of innate needs, with some needs being more powerful than others: the lower the need is in the hierarchy, the more powerful the need is. As the needs are satisfied we are able to move up and concentrate our energies on the next level.

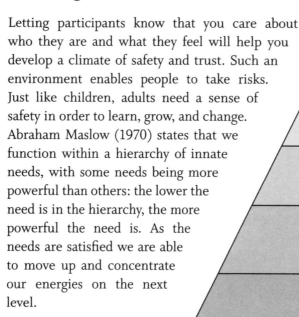

Maslow's Hierarchy of Innate Needs

Physiological Needs and Needs for Safety

Physiological needs are fairly obvious and they come into play during staff development sessions as we plan for comfortable settings, provide food and beverages, and attempt to fulfill people's desire for physical security. Providing safety is fundamental to creating an environment in which people are willing to take risks to learn new things.

One step in creating a safe environment is to let the participants know about the flow of the day and what your expectations are for their participation. A written agenda (whether on a handout or on a posted chart) provides participants with a time frame of what will be happening. Important comfort issues, such as when there will be breaks or how the participants are expected to take care of their personal needs, are essential to address. If it's a longer session, we find that discussing lunch plans at the beginning of the day puts everyone at ease. Physical and emotional comfort is a precursor to feeling safe, which means feeling as though you have some control over your experiences.

The physical setting also creates a sense of safety, so keep comfort in mind when planning for any staff development opportunity. Simple things such as providing comfortable chairs and tables, and arranging them to create a more intimate environment that is safe for taking risks are important. When you can, provide snacks and drinks, and always have water available.

Belonging, Esteem, and Self-Actualization

The next two levels in Maslow's hierarchy of needs—belonging and esteem—are a direct result of feeling accepted by others. This fosters a sense of personal competence and adequacy, which lays the foundation for achieving the final stage of self-actualization. The key factor in helping staff move through these steps is building a sense of trust with you and with each other. Developing trust in both our personal and professional relationships takes time. When people begin to share with others in a safe environment, they begin to develop a sense of trust. As people feel safe, anxiety lessens and that's when learning is most effective. Maslow talks about this need to lessen anxiety: "Spontaneous growth will occur only in an environment which minimizes anxiety and maximizes the delights of growth" (Maslow 1962).

Building Trust in Group Settings ~ Whether you are working with an unfamiliar group or with your colleagues, you can create a more trusting environment by starting off with something as simple as a fun opening activity or a group sharing activity. Here are some ideas:

- In an unfamiliar group, have each participant pair up with someone else, interview that person, and introduce her to the group. (For the sake of time, you may want to specify three or four questions that they should ask each other and use as their introduction, for example, their name, where they are from, and how long they have worked with children.)
- In a familiar group of colleagues, have each person share something about themselves that the others might not know.
- In either type of group, have each person share favorite movies, songs, or television shows.
- In either type of group, have each person share ways that they take good care of themselves—what nourishes them.
- In either type of group, have each person share their favorite thing to do with the children.

We are sure you can add your own favorite opening activities to this list. Use one of these activities in your sessions before you begin to talk about more difficult topics, such as participants' goals or concerns.

We seek to build trust as group facilitators and mentors by sharing a little about our own personal lives as we introduce ourselves to teachers. We try to find connection with the experiences of the group and make it clear that we are not there to lecture, but to join with the participants in a learning process.

We say things like, "I look forward to engaging in a conversation with you and hearing your stories about working with children." We also share our own stories about our teaching experiences, including when we struggled with an issue in our teaching, so that we show our own vulnerability and connect with our participants.

Trust and Power Issues ~ Essential to building a trusting relationship is being sensitive to power issues. Eve Trook developed a model of looking at the ways we use power with children. We have found this to be very effective as we consider adult learning. Trook defines the following possible uses of power:

- *Power ON*: The person has no real choice, i.e., the person is oppressed.
- *Power FOR*: The person is provided experiences that contribute to the development of self-esteem and confidence that lead to power for the person, i.e., the person is facilitated.
- *Power WITH*: The person and the teacher (staff development leader, coach, mentor) are equals, learning together, and the person acquires new power, i.e., all participants are liberated (Trook 1983).

The critical difference between these three possible uses of power is the amount of control the leader takes. In using *Power ON,* the leader has total control. Using *Power FOR* means the leader is intentionally guiding, structuring, or supporting learners toward a goal. Using *Power WITH* means that both the learners and the leader share as equals in the learning process. The more we can create a sense of wonder, delight, and accomplishment together, the more empowered teachers become in the process of change and the more likely the changes will be integrated into their daily practices. If our efforts in this difficult process of change and implementation of standards and other issues of accountability are to be successful we must provide ways to empower the participants.

"[T]he human organism needs a climate of trust and support in order to grow. People cannot risk changing without trust" (Morgan 1983, 14). It is important to keep in mind that the process of change is gradual and that some resistance to integrating new information is positive—in fact, it can be seen as a necessary part of the process. You might want to refer back to the change continuum on page 23 as you find ways to balance the need for change with the existing concerns of the teachers.

Helping Others Keep Their Passion for Their Work with Young Children

In our experience we have found that in an atmosphere of acceptance teachers will begin to willingly share their joys and passions in their work with children. We often have them create lists of the things that they most enjoy about their jobs. We then refer back to those lists to build other activities so that we are continuing to connect to the participants' delight in their work. We have found that as teachers consider integrating standards, they are worried about having to give up what they enjoy the most. Many have told us that they are worried about having to let go of music, art, or outside time in the quest for a more academic program and they are also concerned about having to fit something more into their already busy days. In planning for staff development, then, our job becomes one of helping teachers to see how they can implement standards through the things that they love in ways that are developmentally appropriate for the children.

There are staff development activities and coaching suggestions in chapters 4 through 8 to help you do this, including:

- leading discussions that help teachers discover how many of the activities that they are already doing with children fit into the new criteria—which lessens teachers' concerns about "doing more"
- identifying how many academic activities are imbedded in daily routines
- addressing assessment issues by showing the ways that observations help teachers to track progress toward a standard

Play for Adults and the Parallel Process

In our staff development sessions, we consciously model developmentally appropriate practices, showing how we want the adults to work with children. Just as we want teachers to provide environments for children that are inclusive of best practices, we need to create learning environments for adults that are rich in opportunities to grow and learn as well, full of opportunities to learn through play and exploration. Valuing the importance of play for children, we must provide opportunities for adults to be playful in their learning. We need to "practice what we preach."

Elizabeth Jones (1997, xi) states: "[W]e don't stop learning through play just because we are grown up. Learning through play includes playing with the possibilities, being flexible, staying loose when things go wrong, being curious, thinking creatively, and problem solving. . . . Teachers of young children should be taught in the same way I hope they will teach. . . . adults [should] be treated according to the developmental principles they must follow in working with young children. Good teachers are playful; they don't take themselves too seriously." In planning for staff development activities, we take these recommendations very much to heart.

We do not believe that staff development sessions should be only lecture oriented, with participants as passive receivers of information. The following information (Carter and Curtis 1994, 243) helps us plan for a variety of activities:

> *People remember:*
> *10% of what they read*
> *20% of what they hear*
> *30% of what they see*
> *50% of what they hear and see*
> *70% of what they say or write*
> *90% of what they say as they do a thing.*

The implications of this list are astounding! As we attend national and state early childhood conferences, we are very surprised to see that many sessions are still offered using the traditional format of lecture, even though it's clear that this is one of the least effective ways to learn. Doing and saying remain the most effective ways to incorporate new information. So we strongly recommend that staff development leaders change to a more active-learning approach for adults to insure that information is retained and used.

We do recognize the need to present ideas and we even use PowerPoint slides to do so. (We've provided some of those slides on the CD included in this book for you to use with your staff development activities.) However, we attempt to keep such presentations of information to a short time period and then offer time for participants to play with the ideas that were shared. How do they play? Through discussion with each other, through trying something out, and through relating to personal experiences and being given the opportunity to tell their own stories. We offer ways for them to represent their thinking—on charts, through skits, or through group presentations. We have them work in small groups and also come back together to share with the large group. We try to pace our sessions so that the flow of activities includes opportunities for listening as well as lots of opportunities for talking and doing. All of this is our interpretation of the parallel process. And we are thrilled when a participant comments, "I see what you're doing. You've set up this session just like we would plan activities for the children!"

Just as children come to us with a variety of life experiences, so do adults. Adults bring to the learning process a complex mix of experiences, knowledge, and skills as well as preset attitudes about themselves, teaching, and the topic. So while the process of learning is the same, adults add a degree of complexity based on their more extensive life experiences. Therefore, in planning activities for adults we must take this into account. We may ask teachers to play with materials the way the children do—but we also ask them to think about what they are doing as adults. They can identify the learning that is inherent as children use these materials. They can analyze early learning standards and see where the standards are being addressed. That's adding the complexity and asking them to use their knowledge and experience in a playful way. We have tried to model the parallel process in the many activities we provide in this book.

Addressing Different Learning Styles and Experiences

We all have seen that adults, like children, learn in different ways. Learning is a reflection of each person's culture, life experiences, and personality. The work of Howard Gardner provides us with a framework for understanding that learning occurs in different ways for different people. His theory identifies the following multiple intelligences:

- Intrapersonal Intelligence—recognizing how one's own emotions impact behavior
- Interpersonal Intelligence—recognizing and understanding the moods, intentions, and emotions of others
- Linguistic Intelligence—understanding the function of language, being sensitive to its sound and rhythm
- Logical-Mathematical Intelligence—being able to see and understand numerical and logical patterns
- Spatial Intelligence—being able to see the spatial world and being able to re-create what one has observed
- Musical Intelligence—appreciating the qualities of musical expression
- Bodily-Kinesthetic Intelligence—using the body for expression
- Naturalistic Intelligence—understanding and using the relationships in nature (Gardner 1983)

Looking at the different types of intelligences helps us to understand how people acquire information in the most meaningful ways. Unfortunately, in many educational settings, the primary focus is on the logical-mathematical and linguistic intelligences. If someone is not as strong in these two ways of thinking, she may not be as successful in the learning opportunities presented. If we incorporate Gardner's theory and plan staff development activities that incorporate more than one or two ways of learning, we will be providing opportunities for each participant to maximize her learning potential.

In our staff development planning we try to include activities that address as many of Gardner's intelligences as we can. Linguistic intelligence is engaged through a variety of ways, including verbal presentations, PowerPoint slides, and handouts. The design of the slides and handouts incorporates logical-mathematical intelligence in the way key points are outlined and illustrated. We invite participants to do lots of discussion in small groups or in pairs or triads so that interpersonal intelligence is valued. And we give the participants opportunities to represent their discussions and express their ideas in many forms, including drawings or group posters, charts, diagrams, poems, and raps, as well as dancing, singing, and acting things out.

Culture and personality affect learning styles as well. Many people learn best in small group discussions in response to a thought-provoking question or idea. While some people feel comfortable speaking up in a large group, many people don't. They may be shyer than or not as verbal as others. They may be observers and listeners who like to take in information and ponder it, or they may be influenced by cultural expectations and experiences. The language of the workshop may not be their first language. Or they may feel uncomfortable with the cultural dynamics of the group. It is important to have a variety of learning activities that reflect these differences in not only learning style but comfort level. We try for a balance between both large and small group activities to insure that all participants have an opportunity to have their voices heard. And we try to be sensitive to cultural and language issues as well.

A Teacher's Stage of Professional Development Affects Learning

Another factor to keep in mind is the developmental stage of each teacher's experience in working with children. As we plan for groups of participants we try to remember that any group of teachers may include individuals who are brand-new to the field as well as ones with years of experience with children. Activities should provide the capability to address the needs at differing developmental levels. Mary Nolan (2007) shares the following developmental stages of teachers and makes recommendations regarding the learning needs at each stage:

- *Survival*—This is the developmental stage of new teachers, usually in their first year of teaching. They often feel inadequate and unprepared for the daily challenges that they face.
- *Consolidation*—During this stage, teachers, usually in their second or third year, are beginning to feel that they have the skills to survive daily life and have mastered some teaching skills.
- *Renewal*—Teachers during this stage, in their fourth, fifth, or sixth years, are beginning to need new ideas to try. They are ready to take on new ideas and benefit from attending conferences and having time with peers.
- *Maturity*—Usually year seven and beyond, these teachers have a high level of self-understanding and of their professional role, and often begin to work on acquiring a more advanced knowledge base.

In addition, Lilian Katz identifies the learning needs that are most prevalent at each stage. The earlier teachers are in their teaching career, the more important coaching and mentoring become. The later they are in their teaching career, the more beneficial ongoing study and staff development sessions become. The following table illustrates these needs.

Stages of Development and Training Needs of Preschool Teachers

Developmental Stages	Learning Needs					
Stage IV				➡ Seminars, institutes, courses, degree programs, books, journals, conferences		
Stage III			➡ Conferences, professional associations, journals, magazines, films, visits to demonstration projects			
Stage II		➡ On-site assistance, access to specialists, colleague advice, consultants				
Stage I	➡ On-site support and technical assistance					
	0	1 YR.	2 YR.	3 YR.	4 YR.	5 YR.

Katz, Lilian. 2005. The developmental stages of teachers. http://ceep.crc.uiuc.edu/pubs/katz-dev-stages.html. Reprinted with permission.

Providing Ongoing Learning Opportunities

Teachers need time to try out new ideas. They need opportunities to make mistakes and learn from them. Sometimes, fear of not doing things right becomes a barrier. We are sure all teachers can remember a time when they were reluctant to try something new because they feared making a mistake and being judged for it. Many of us have very high expectations for ourselves and may feel reluctant to try some new idea or strategy, fearing that we will not do it perfectly. We try to assure the participants with whom we work that it is all right to not be perfect the first time they try something new. Then, in follow-up sessions, we address the successes and challenges that they experienced. We have found that this process of coming together, learning something new, going out and trying it in the classroom, and coming back for fine-tuning is the most effective approach for change to occur. This also emphasizes the importance of reflection: taking the time to consciously think about how a new activity or idea worked and what changes might be needed.

Opportunities to try things out can be provided during staff development sessions using video vignettes and case studies of real-life examples of children in action. Many of our activities in chapters 4 through 7 include the use of video vignettes and case studies. Most valuable, though, are discussions of teachers' own experiences with children. If an atmosphere of trust has been established, sharing of personal successes and challenges can be beneficial for all participants.

Putting New Ideas into Practice

We believe providing new information and ideas through multiple staff development sessions with follow-up coaching and mentoring in the classroom is the most effective model for learning and making changes. We have all been to workshops with dynamic and knowledgeable presenters and left all fired up and ready to implement new ideas. But in reality, by the time we were back in our day-to-day lives with children, we found it very difficult, if not impossible, to implement the good ideas that we had learned. The carryover from one experience is not as long-lasting as that from multiple learning experiences. Teachers need someone to walk along beside them as they try to implement new teaching ideas and strategies. By adding opportunities for individual mentoring and coaching, the focus changes to the needs of the individual. The mentor/coach and the teacher make decisions together regarding how the change process will be implemented. We see this as an opportunity to use the *Power WITH* approach discussed on page 32.

Going into classrooms as a coach and mentor allows you to individualize your work to meet each teacher's needs and work with her personality and teaching style. It encourages her to show you how she is making attempts to integrate the concepts and ideas explored in staff development sessions. It also gives you the opportunity to see the challenges she is facing with specific children, classroom management, or the flow of her daily routine. You not only observe, but can also model and demonstrate alternate approaches as you spend time with the children and her. You are now part of her process of trying things out.

We have found that spending a minimum of forty-five minutes to one hour observing, followed by at least thirty minutes in a reflective conversation with the teacher, works well. You may not always be able to converse with the teacher immediately after the observation. In that case, schedule the reflection time as soon as possible after your time in the classroom. We find that it helps to give the teacher some positive feedback immediately after the observation to relieve possible anxiety. For example, saying something as simple as, "I've really enjoyed being in your classroom" may help.

Another Set of Eyes—Documentation as a Coaching Technique ~ We find that coaching in classrooms is hard work. It is easy to fall into the role of "the expert" who tells the teacher how to work with specific children or facilitate activities. If we tell people how to do something, they may do it, but they will best understand it if they've constructed their knowledge for themselves. This is where using direct observation of the children (rather than the teacher you're coaching) and documenting what you see can be useful. As class coaches, we have written down descriptions of the children's actions and documented their comments. The teacher can then use the descriptions and comments for their observational assessment documentation. In this way, we are providing another set of eyes and ears in the classroom, and recording children's actions for reflection and discussion in the coaching session. In addition, we have documented what the children are doing by writing a story that describes their play. It could be a story that describes a dramatic play scene that the children have created, or it could be a description of their creations with playdough. The children love to see their names in print and pay close attention as the story is read. They usually run to their teacher and share it with her. This gives her an opportunity to celebrate and support their actions. It also models for her ways to take the children's experiences to another level—that of representation through literacy to be shared with others. Some coaches take photographs of the children and post them with the descriptive stories. Again, this can be a model to the teacher of ways to capture documentation for assessment as well as display purposes.

Building in Time for Reflection

We believe in the important role that reflection plays in learning, and we try to build it into any activity that we plan for teachers. Reflection helps people to take new information, strategies, and techniques and make them their own, to integrate them in relevant and meaningful ways that will be different for each person. The reflection process involves making connections to what one already knows.

At the end of a workshop, we provide the participants with questions such as:

- What worked for you?
- What didn't work so well for you?
- What will you be trying differently with the children in your classroom?
- Do you have any concerns or questions?
- What tools and support do you need to have your concerns or questions addressed?
- Is there anything else that you would like us to know?

You may have other questions that you find help participants reflect on their experience in a staff development session.

In addition to answering such questions, ongoing reflection can be done through individual journaling and in meetings with peers, mentors, or coaches. Journaling can give teachers an opportunity to think and reflect on their progress toward incorporating standards and other issues of accountability into daily life with the children. The journal provides a structured experience for teachers to think and write about their process of growth and change. We realize that this takes time, but we think that it is an important and necessary commitment to make for true and lasting change to occur.

The format for reflection through journaling can be answering the same questions that are listed above across time (perhaps once a week or once a month). Then the teacher and her mentor can compare how her responses change over time, enabling the teacher to clearly see her growth.

Ongoing reflection can also be done in verbal debriefing sessions after a classroom observation by a coach through the use of thought-provoking questioning as teachers try out new activities or ideas. We have often begun a reflective dialogue by saying something as simple as "Tell me about _____ " and then using the response as a springboard for further discussion. Another opportunity for verbal reflection is for teachers to meet periodically with another teacher to reflect on how things are going in their classrooms as they integrate new ideas and activities.

Facilitator vs. Evaluator

To be an effective part of the reflection process, mentors or coaches need to make sure that their role is one of facilitator rather than evaluator. If you are a director and need to also evaluate your staff, you will want to make clear which role you are playing when you meet with a teacher. Margie Carter (1993, 51) gives the following suggestions to help you act in the facilitative role:

> *Directors can spend part of their time as facilitators rather than evaluators if*
>
> 1. *they enter classrooms with a focus on children rather than on teachers;*
> 2. *they model an interest in children's play and initiate discussions of it as it's happening;*
> 3. *they "broadcast" their observations throughout the center (using notes, sketches, photos, and audio and videotapes);*
> 4. *they observe for and point out environmental factors that support play; and*
> 5. *they observe for and point out teacher behaviors that encourage sustained play by children—catching teachers "being good."*

Getting Support to Meet the Challenges of This Work

We recognize that when you are in a staff development leadership role, the work you do will continue to challenge you both professionally and personally. As you plan thoughtful and effective ways to support teachers' learning you also must learn to take good care of yourself and to use a reflective process of your own to guide your work. Jones (1997) talks about the need to recognize how our anxiety as the leaders in a situation can potentially interfere with our ability to recognize the anxiety of others. We must develop our own awareness and be careful to think about our feelings as well as those of the participants.

While, in our work, we often ask participants to answer reflective questions as an evaluation tool to determine the success of our efforts, we consider the time we spend individually reflecting or in conversation with co-leaders to be of equal, if not more, importance. Whenever we do any kind of presentation or coaching session, we ask ourselves questions such as:

- What worked well from my perspective?
- What didn't work well?

- What was the level of participation from the group?
- What did the body language of the participants tell me?
- What can I change or do differently next time?

We have learned that having a colleague to talk with is invaluable. We have been working, teaching, and presenting together for many years now. A part of our success and satisfaction comes from our mutual support, which we consider to be vital if we are to continue. We highly recommend that you build a network of support for yourself in your efforts. This communication doesn't have to be face to face. We live in different states—Indiana and Montana—and met teaching online for Pacific Oaks College. Most of our communication is by e-mail or telephone. Yet we continue to have a very successful relationship, both as colleagues and as friends. We are able to provide a continual support network for each other even when we are working on separate projects. It's the sense of connection that makes the difference for us both. We would strongly encourage each one of you to develop a system of support for yourself in this very important work that you do.

So, consider the following questions for yourself:

- What is working well for me?
- What isn't going so well?
- What would I change or do differently?
- And last, but perhaps most important, what support do I need, and from whom, to do my work in the best way possible?

In the next chapter, we will discuss the best ways to implement curricula for young children. We will provide staff development activities to help teachers make changes in their curricular practices.

References

Boeree, George C. Abraham Maslow 1908–1970. Accessed August 16, 2007, at www.ship.edu/~cgboeree.

Carter, Margie. 1993. Catching teachers "being good": Using observation to communicate. In *Growing teachers: Partnerships in staff development*, ed. Elizabeth Jones, 35–53. Washington, D.C.: NAEYC.

Carter, Margie, and Deb Curtis. 1994. *Training teachers: A harvest of theory and practice*. St. Paul: Redleaf Press.

Gardner, Howard. 1983. *Frames of mind: The theory of multiple intelligences*. New York: Basic Books.

Jones, Elizabeth. 1997. *Teaching adults: An active learning approach.* Washington, D.C.: NAEYC.

Katz, Lilian G. The developmental stages of teachers. Accessed May 14, 2007, at http://ceep.crc.uiuc.edu/pubs/katz-dev-stages.html.

Maslow, Abraham H. 1962. *Toward a psychology of being.* New York: Van Norstrand Reinhold.

Maslow, Abraham H. 1970. *Motivation and personality.* New York: Harper and Row.

Morgan, Christina. 1983. Journal of a day care administrator. In *Administration: A bedside guide,* ed. Sharon Stine, 11–14. Pasadena, Calif.: Pacific Oaks College.

Nolan, Mary. 2007. *Mentor coaching and leadership.* Clifton Park, N.Y.: Thompson Delmar Learning.

Trook, Eve. 1983. Understanding teachers' uses of power: A role-playing activity. In *On the growing edge: Notes by college teachers making changes*, ed. Elizabeth Jones, 15–22. Pasadena, Calif.: Pacific Oaks College.

Helping Others Implement Curricula in Ways Best for Young Children

Often early educators and administrators confuse the call for accountability to early learning standards with the need to change curricular practices completely so that teacher-led activities take priority over child-initiated ones. It takes thoughtful planning and intentionality on the part of teachers to address early learning standards as children play and explore, go through daily routines, and participate in large and small group activities. But quality programs across the country are proving that it can be done. In this chapter, we will provide staff development activities that address issues related to play-based curricula. Then, in chapter 5 we will provide activities that help teachers integrate early learning standards in their curricular planning and implementation.

The Complexity of Curriculum for Young Children

Defining and implementing a developmentally appropriate curriculum for young children is complicated, which is why some policymakers and academics want to standardize early learning and institute "measurable," rote, teacher-directed practices. A child-centered curriculum involves constant decisions and adjustments by teachers in response to the children's engagement levels and behavior. The complex nature of such a curriculum arises from the following four factors:

1. It's difficult to define just when learning is occurring.
2. Teaching young children involves devising and using multiple strategies and playing multiple roles to enhance the learning process.

3. The success of learning opportunities cannot be assessed only by measuring children's knowledge, but must also be assessed by considering their level of engagement in activities that are meaningful to them and that are deemed by them to be worthy of their attention and energy.

4. Assessment is an ongoing process integrated with curricular implementation so that the teaching process is also a reflection of the learning process.

In addition to these characteristics, NAEYC is now being much more explicit in its accreditation criteria for curriculum (NAEYC 2006). Here is the rationale given for the curriculum program standard:

A curriculum that draws on research assists teachers in identifying important concepts and skills as well as effective methods for fostering children's learning and development. When informed by teachers' knowledge of individual children, a well-articulated curriculum guides teachers so they can provide children with experiences that foster growth across a broad range of developmental and content areas. A curriculum also helps ensure that the teacher is intentional in planning a daily schedule that (a) maximizes children's learning through effective use of time, materials used for play, self-initiated learning, and creative expression as well as (b) offers opportunities for children to learn individually and in groups according to their developmental needs and interests.

Some teachers and directors are concerned that the lack of a defined curriculum meeting these criteria may hurt their chances at receiving accreditation in the future. We believe that curricular practices can be more clearly articulated so that early educators will see how much they are already doing that reflects the complexity of an effective preschool curriculum and meets accreditation standards. In this chapter, we will look at many aspects of a preschool curriculum and provide four staff development activities (numbered 1 through 4) that address the following:

- the appropriateness and importance of play and daily routines as the primary activities for young children's learning
- appropriate teaching strategies that support productive child engagement and learning

For each of the staff development activities, we will reference PowerPoint slides. For some of the activities, we will also provide handouts or case studies that you can use. The handouts and case studies can be found in appendixes

A and B, respectively, as well as on the CD accompanying this book. You will need to make your copies from the CD. The PowerPoint slides are also on the CD.

In chapter 8, we will look at various forms of resistance that teachers may demonstrate as they attempt to make the recommended changes in their curriculum. We will offer you coaching strategies to help you address these forms of resistance and encourage teachers to embrace new ideas about curriculum for young children.

Learning through Play and Daily Routines

The field of early childhood education has long recognized that children learn through play and exploration. There is much research to support this view of young children's learning. In appendix E, we provide an article written by Dolores Stegelin in which she cites numerous research studies that support the importance of play as the vehicle for learning in the early years. Should you need to explain to others the importance and validity of learning through play, you can use the research cited in this article.

As you work with teachers around the topic of curriculum, you will want to remind them that as children play, explore, and investigate, they are gaining skills and knowledge. They may be practicing and refining what they already know how to do: for example, using their small muscles to snap together plastic blocks or using their spatial thinking to put together puzzle pieces. They may be problem solving as they stack blocks in a tower or as they negotiate a dramatic play script with other players. These kinds of activities are essential components in an early childhood curriculum, and a teacher's direct interaction is not necessary for learning to occur. The teacher is involved by planning the environment. She provides materials and organizes the choices for the children. She is ready with help and support if needed. Yet, she does not have to instruct or directly intervene to facilitate the children's learning. Instead, she sets up the possibilities for such learning to occur.

You will also want to help teachers remember that daily routines are part of curriculum as well. Snacks and meals, hand washing and toileting, arrival and departure, and transitioning can be times when learning is occurring. For example, children can be developing literacy skills while in the bathroom washing their hands. They recognize "H" for hot and "C" for cold or the signs for "Girls" or "Boys." They learn to follow sequential directions for applying soap, scrubbing, rinsing, and drying. They engage in conversations that support their oral language development. They learn to button and snap for themselves, working not only on fine motor skills, but also on independence and self-help.

Packaged Curricula and Curriculum Frameworks

The fact that children are learning through play and participation in daily routines is hard to capture in a curriculum if it's defined too narrowly. Publishers have funded the development of packaged curricula that offer selections of books, hands-on materials, and teacher manuals that provide lesson plans across the school year. Some of these packaged curricula also include scripts for teachers to follow when interacting with children. These prescribed plans and scripts can provide a starting point for learning but need to be implemented with careful attention not only to the needs of each child but also to the unique nature of each classroom. No prepackaged set of scripted activities can possibly address the varied learning styles and dispositions of individual children or reflect the special characteristics of programs and the diversity of families and communities without adaptations by the teachers using them.

On the other hand, commonly used child-centered curricular frameworks such as the Creative Curriculum, High/Scope Curriculum, the Project Approach, and the Reggio Emilia approach, go beyond a scripted set of activities. Each of these recommends a more open-ended style to implementing curriculum based on a carefully planned environment that is responsive to the children's interests. These frameworks and approaches recognize that the child brings much to the learning experience that influences the decisions the teacher makes. A curricular package cannot capture the learning that occurs during play and routines in ways that the more open-ended frameworks and approaches can. No matter what curriculum you are using, it's important to recognize and attend to the differences in children's learning needs, styles, and timetables. Relating that learning to early learning standards adds another dimension of complexity.

What Is Teaching? Identifying Teaching Strategies

We believe that it is helpful to remind teachers of the many forms that teaching can take. Beyond planning for children's choices within the environment and daily routines, there are many other opportunities for teaching to occur. For example, teachers can

- facilitate children's interactions with each other and with adults

- enhance children's learning by adding vocabulary words to conversations and helping them follow through with plans and sequences
- validate and celebrate what children are doing as they accomplish tasks or come up with new ideas
- redirect children's actions so that their engagement stays productive
- scaffold children's learning by providing assistance when they cannot do something independently yet
- build on children's topics of interest by planning in-depth projects and studies

Teaching young children is layered with opportunities that go far beyond direct instruction alone. Early educators must make the most of every minute with the children to intentionally and purposefully enhance the learning potential of situations throughout each and every day.

What a teacher does when children explore or participate in daily routines may look quite different from what she does when leading a small or large group activity. No matter what curricular package or approach is being used, she has a wide range of choices that extend from nonintervening support and encouragement to direct instruction. The following continuum from *Reaching Potentials: Appropriate Curriculum and Assessment for Young Children, Vol. 1* (Bredekamp and Rosegrant 1992) has been adapted to attempt to capture this range of teaching options. The continuum also shows the child's level of engagement related to the teaching strategies that are used to enhance the child's learning. Note that the more directive a teacher is, the more passive the child is. In the early childhood years, children learn best through active engagement. Therefore, less directive strategies should be used most frequently for the curriculum to be effective for young children.

Teaching Continuum

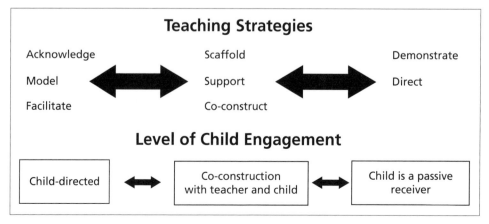

A teacher has to figure out which level of intervention is most appropriate in multiple situations throughout the day. On-the-spot decisions must be made and interventions tried and immediately evaluated to determine their success in enhancing the learning of the child. If teachers wore a strip of masking tape hanging down from their belts and made a hash mark each time they made such a spontaneous decision regarding their level of engagement with a child, they would end up with hundreds of hash marks at the end of a day! Teachers engage in continual decision making regarding the most effective strategies to use with each child in each situation.

In Staff Development Activity 1, "Identifying Teaching Strategies," we suggest that you use the continuum from page 48 and have teachers analyze case studies taken directly from classroom experiences. We provide several case studies in appendix B for you to use. These case studies could also be used to help teachers determine ways to create curricular activities that engage children in active learning as well as assess their progress and capabilities. We invite you to use the case studies in ways that work best for your purposes.

Staff Development Activity 1

Identifying Teaching Strategies

Purpose: To consider the range of teaching strategies and interventions that may be most effective in a variety of situations with children.

What to Do: See PowerPoint slides 1–5. See handouts 1a, 1b, and 1c.

Using the Teaching Continuum (provided in handout 1a), look at a case study of a classroom incident. We have provided here one incident to analyze in this way. (It is also provided in handout 1b.) Other case studies are provided in appendix B. Instead of case studies you may wish to use incidents that have occurred in your teachers' classrooms. Have the participants read through the case study or incident and then join in a group discussion as outlined on page 50.

Case Study
Throwing Colored Bears

Three four-year-old boys are invited by their teacher to sort colored bears into round sorting trays with multiple compartments. As long as the teacher is there with them, the boys cooperate in the sorting activity, talking about the colors of the bears as they sort them. As she moves on after five or six minutes to help in another area of the classroom, their interaction with the bears changes. "Hey, I know," says Alec. "Let's see who can throw them into the tray!" The boys move the trays to the opposite end of the table and begin to throw the bears. Their initial throws involve aiming at the small compartments. As bears fly across the table and land in the compartments, some of them bounce out again onto the table from the force of the throw. The boys laugh hysterically and continue to throw the bears harder and harder. Their laughter grows louder by the minute. Soon, bears are flying across the table and onto the floor. The boys' laughter is high-pitched. They pound on and lie across the table as each bear lands.

Group Discussion: Ask the participants to refer to the Teaching Continuum and identify the possible teaching strategies that a teacher might use to enhance the situation most fully for the children. It is more than likely that the participants will recognize that multiple strategies could be used depending on the particular reactions of the children. The discussion can focus on how much intervention is needed on the part of the teacher to help these boys continue to work with the bears in a way that is productive and related to learning.

The following are some possible choices that teachers could make depending on their goal and the reactions of the boys involved. (These choices are also provided in handout 1c.)

If the goal is Safety, the teacher may choose to Facilitate: You move toward the boys, reminding them to take good care of materials and not hurt each other. You stay nearby to make sure that they tone down their throwing.

If the goal is to Sustain the boys' interest and be safe, the teacher may choose to Model: You move toward the boys, reminding them to take good care of materials and not hurt each other. You sit down with them and offer suggestions to help them aim more carefully and throw more gently so that the bears land in the compartments. You might say things like: "What would happen if you threw your bears more gently? Will they stay in the compartment? Should we pull the tray a little closer and try that? Or would it help to move it to the floor and drop the bears from a standing position? How can we make this safer?"

If the goal is to Extend what they are doing, the teacher may choose to Scaffold and Support: You move toward the boys and ask, "How many bears will this particular compartment hold? Shall we count and see?" As the play calms down and more careful aim is taken, you introduce purpose to the actions that goes beyond just throwing. "I wonder how many bears you can drop or throw gently into this compartment." You stay with the boys to get this going and help them count. You watch closely to see if they take the play in this direction and do calm down.

If the goal is to Interrupt because the play does not calm down, the teacher may choose to Direct: You introduce some different ways to use the bears and sorting trays. "We need to stop throwing the bears because this is not safe. I'm afraid our sorting trays will get broken or someone in our room will get hit by a bear." You can then suggest other ways to use the bears and sorting trays. "Let's go back to sitting at the table and sorting the bears into the tray. Shall we sort by color or by size? I see little bears, medium bears, and big bears. I also see lots of different colors. Which way should we sort them?" You stay with the boys to get this going and help them sort. You watch closely to see if they take the play in this direction and do calm down.

If the goal is to Enrich and engage them for an even longer period of time, the teacher may choose to Co-construct: You can offer them a challenge. In the case of a sorting activity, one next step is to create patterns. You can model a simple pattern with two different colors of bears or two different sizes of bears in a repeating sequence. As you build your pattern, you say, "I'm going to challenge you! Can you figure out what I need to put next in my line of bears? Do you see how the color or size repeats? Can you make a line of bears like that?" You have now engaged them intellectually so that they are moving to higher levels of thinking and application of knowledge.

• • • • • ⊙ • • • •

Activities that Engage

Identifying the qualities of activities that successfully engage children is another way to determine the effectiveness of curricular strategies. Staff Development Activity 2, "Engaging Children in Learning," gives you ideas about how to explore child engagement with teachers.

Staff Development Activity 2
. . . .

Engaging Children in Learning

Purpose: To help teachers identify the characteristics of children's actions, facial expressions, and verbal comments that show they find an activity engaging and to evaluate activities for levels of child engagement.

What to Do: See PowerPoint slide 6. See handout 1a.

In small groups, have teachers generate a list of ways that they know children are actively engaged in a learning situation. The list might include things like:

- The children are working with materials productively.
- They stay focused on the task for an extended period of time.
- Their eyes are bright and their general affect is of happiness, enjoyment, or satisfaction.
- They come up with new ideas on how to do something.
- They volunteer information or share their thinking with others.
- They make connections to their own experiences, showing that the activity has meaning for them.

You may want to begin the list and ask the group to add to it.

Group Discussion: Have the groups share their lists and give examples of times and activities in their classrooms when the children were showing these characteristics. In this sharing, you may notice that the teachers exhibit many of the same characteristics that children do when they are actively engaged. Teachers may be smiling, their eyes bright as they share these successful times with their young charges.

Next, ask the teachers to identify the teaching strategies that they used in the activities identified as engaging. For example, perhaps one of the examples was a description of children's work with a marble run. Have the members of the group discuss what teaching strategies were used to facilitate and sustain the children's engagement in building and using the run. Then note where those teaching strategies would fall on the Teaching Continuum (see handout 1a). More than likely, they will fall in the left and middle columns, where the children are self-directed or in collaboration with a teacher.

• • • • • ◉ • • • • •

Balancing Teacher-Directed and Child-Initiated Activities

We believe that the goal of curriculum is to actively engage the children so that they will expend effort, stay with a task, relate it to prior learning, and take risks to learn something new. The choice of teaching strategies, then, will be critical to the success of that curriculum. Young children are egocentric and have high energy levels. Therefore, they respond best to opportunities where they can choose activities. Yet, they still need adult guidance to keep their self-initiation positive and productive. Elizabeth Jones and Gretchen Reynolds (1992, 1) state: "Young children learn the most important things not by being told but by constructing knowledge for themselves in interaction with the physical world and with other children—and the way they do this is by playing." Finding the right balance of child direction and adult guidance is the challenge. The goal is to promote children's engagement, rather than have it deteriorate into chaotic, out of control play, conflict, or unproductive use of time, energy, or materials. When a teacher is intentionally trying to enhance learning for children and integrate early learning standards, she needs to be very cognizant of this balance and should strive to have it be more heavily weighted on the child-initiated play side than on the teacher-directed one.

To help teachers think more deeply about this balance, Staff Development Activity 3, "Breathing Out and Breathing In," suggests that teachers analyze daily schedules and figure out ways to make adaptations so that teacher-led activities take up far less time than those that are child-initiated.

Staff Development Activity 3

Breathing Out and Breathing In

Purpose: To think about activities in terms of children's active or passive engagement and analyze daily schedules to determine the balance between the two.

What to Do: See PowerPoint slides 7–9. See handouts 2a and 2b.

Share the ideas from Sylvia Ashton-Warner (1963) regarding children's need to "breathe out" before they are asked to "breathe in" (see handout 2a). Breathing out involves any form of self-expression: talking, moving, creating, dancing, singing, building, drawing, or writing. The child is active, in charge, taking the lead, and physically expressing feelings, thoughts, ideas, or experiences in some way. Breathing in, on the other hand, is more passive in nature. The child is taking in information, listening, observing, pondering, or considering.

Then have teachers review the daily schedule in handout 2b and look at their own daily schedules to analyze the flow of activities.

Group Discussion: Discuss ways that breathing out and breathing in are seen in the schedules. Ask the following question: "Does the schedule allow children to express themselves in activity and conversation before it asks them to settle down and listen?" If teachers are reporting that their large or small group times are difficult and children are not paying attention, the reason may very well be that children did not have an opportunity to "breathe out" enough before the group began. Discuss possible changes to the daily schedule and even to the structure of the group time.

• • • • • ◉ • • • •

Sustaining Children's Play

We find it helpful to engage teachers in discussions about sustaining children's play. Jones and Reynolds (1992) suggest that to make the most of children's play and self-initiation, teachers must work to sustain the play rather than interrupt it. They point out that for safety's sake (and possibly other reasons) interruption may be the choice a teacher must make at times. However, they caution teachers to think about the way that interruption is handled. They use the language from Eve Trook referred to on page 32 and suggest that rather than interrupting play and exhibiting *Power ON* the children, teachers instead interrupt in a way that works *FOR* and *WITH* the children: "*Power ON* is appropriate and necessary when safety is involved. . . . But *Power ON* ignores and interrupts play. Effective facilitation—*Power FOR*—takes the script and rhythm of the play into account, even when there are conflicts to be solved" (Jones and Reynolds 1992, 50). How does a teacher know when the teaching strategy or intervention she has chosen is interrupting the play or sustaining it? By building on the play so that the children take over and the play becomes focused and extended. The children's engagement will show through in their bright eyes, happy affect, and involvement in the task at hand.

> When in doubt, trust the play. It is the children's curriculum. Play that is scattered or potentially disruptive may require refocusing, but well-focused, complex play requires no intervention. . . . Adults who interrupt play, whatever their reasons, are usually in so much of a hurry that they fail to pay attention to children's purposes. SLOW DOWN is advice to keep in mind. We shortchange young children when we hurry them. We learn most about them, and help them learn most, when we pay attention to what is happening for them as they play (Jones and Reynolds 1992, 56).

Staff Development Activity 4, "When to Sustain and When to Interrupt," addresses this issue.

Staff Development Activity 4

When to Sustain and When to Interrupt

Purpose: To determine teacher interactions with children that sustain their engagement in activities and interactions that interrupt it.

What to Do: See PowerPoint slides 10–12. See handout 3.

Have the participants read through the following two scenarios (provided in handout 3) and determine whether the teacher is sustaining children's engagement or interrupting it.

Scenario 1
Magic Capes

Three boys and one girl (all four-year-olds) are playing in the dramatic play area, putting scarves around their backs and calling them "magic capes." Ms. Denise helps them to tie the scarves and asks them, "Why are the scarves magic?" Jacob responds, "Because they make us fly!" and proceeds to laugh loudly and run around the room. Eli and Luis follow him, bumping into each other, while Alejandra watches quietly. Ms. Denise says, "If you boys don't settle down, we'll have to take the scarves away. Why don't you come over here and play with Alejandra? I know! Your magic capes could be magic chef capes to help you cook a wonderful dinner." The boys continue to run around the room and Alejandra remains where she is.

Scenario 2
Test Crash

Several three- and four-year-old children are seated at a table building with Duplos. Robbie and Bryce announce that they are making jet fighters and crash their constructions into one another, destroying them, and laughing. They then grab the pieces and build their "fighters" again. Teacher Racquel sits down and says, "Hey, tell me what's going on over here? What are you building?" Janie says, "I'm building a house." Racquel asks, "Where's the door? Oh, there it is. Who lives in your house, Janie?" As she and Janie talk, Robbie and Bryce crash their fighters again. Racquel says, "Boy, your fighters keep breaking apart when they crash. I wonder if there's a way to build them so that they are stronger. Did you know that the men and women who build airplanes have to work very hard to make their planes so that they are safe? How could you make your planes so that they are safe?" Racquel helps the boys choose parts and then test the connections and sturdiness without crashing. She explains that it's too expensive to do a crash test every time. The engineers have to do other kinds of tests. She then suggests that they take photographs of their different designs so they can remember them and display them for others to see. All of the children at the table start building their constructions and asking her to photograph them. They become much more interested in this aspect of the play and the crashing stops.

Group Discussion: Ask participants to share their thoughts about the scenarios. If the group determines that the teacher interrupted the children's engagement, invite discussion about what next steps could be taken to either refocus the children or to introduce them to something that would be more engaging and worthy of their attention.

After you have the group discuss the intervention strategies in each of these situations, ask them to divide into small groups (no more than four people in a group) and plan two role plays of their own: one demonstrating a teacher interrupting children's play and one demonstrating a teacher sustaining the play. Then, as the groups perform their role plays, ask the members of the large group to identify the strategies that the teacher is using and discuss whether it helps children to remain engaged or not.

• • • • • ◉ • • • • •

These four staff development activities provide you with possibilities for helping teachers think intentionally regarding the aspects of play-based curricula, child engagement, and effective teaching strategies. In the next chapter, staff development activities will be given that address the integration of curriculum and early learning standards.

References:

Ashton-Warner, Sylvia. 1963. *Teacher.* New York: Simon & Schuster.

Bredekamp, Sue, and Teresa Rosegrant, eds. 1992. *Reaching potentials: Appropriate curriculum and assessment for young children,* vol. 1. Washington, D. C.: NAEYC.

Jones, Elizabeth, and Gretchen Reynolds. 1992. The play's the thing: Teachers' roles in children's play. New York: Teachers College Press.

NAEYC Early Childhood Program Standards. Standard 2: NAEYC Accreditation Criteria for Curriculum. 2006. Accessed May 28, 2007, at www.naeyc.org/academy/standards/standard2/.

Stegelin, Dolores A. 2005. Making the case for play policy: Research-based reasons to support play-based environments. *Young Children* 60(2):76–85.

The Integration of Curriculum and Early Learning Standards

The complexity of implementing curricula for young children is increased by the need to integrate early learning standards. As calls for greater accountability to the standards of each state become more common, teachers are working hard to figure out strategies to implement standards within play-based curricula.

This process is a reflection process. It is through continual observation and assessment that teaching strategies are identified. Curriculum and assessment cannot be separated. The cycle here shows the integration of the two.

This cycle helps teachers recognize the ongoing and dynamic nature of teaching young children. Having teachers write down the questions that arise in their minds as they implement a particular activity can lead them to think about this process and become reflective in their practice. Using reflection meetings after classroom observations to dialogue about what was seen and identify next steps will add to the quality of curricular implementation and planning. And bringing in early learning

The Assessment and Curriculum Process

1 Observe and document what you see *(evaluate your plan)*

2 For an individual child: Ask *"What can I do to help this child?"*
For the whole group: Ask *"What is working? What is not?"*

3 Formulate a plan

4 Implement a plan

standards to this cycle of planning and observation enriches and deepens the conversation. In this chapter we provide eight staff development activities (numbered 5 through 12) that address the integration of curriculum and early learning standards. For each of the staff development activities, we will reference PowerPoint slides. For some of the activities, we will also provide handouts or case studies, or refer to video vignettes that you can use. The handouts and case studies can be found in appendixes A and B, respectively, as well as on the CD accompanying this book. You will want to make your copies from the CD. The PowerPoint slides are also on the CD. The video vignettes can be found on the accompanying DVD.

As teachers think about integrating early learning standards into activities (whether they be child-directed play and daily routines or teacher-led group times), they have two choices:

1. Will they observe and think about how the standards were reflected naturally in the activities?
2. Or will they intentionally plan to address a specific set of standards in an activity?

Natural and Intentional Integration

Addressing early learning standards as they are reflected naturally in children's play requires intimate knowledge of the early learning standards and time to reflect on what children did in relation to them. Teachers may document in written anecdotes children's dramatic play interactions or their work with puzzles so that they can remember just what each child did. Conversations among colleagues can center on what each person observed children doing that day. Together, then, teachers determine what early learning standards they saw evidenced in the children's engagement in activities throughout the day. To be successful with a natural approach to integrating early learning standards into curriculum, a teacher must be open and ready for children to show her what they know and can do.

When intentionally integrating early learning standards into a curriculum, a teacher may plan an activity with an early learning standard in mind. She is intentional about the materials chosen and has identified clear goals for that activity. The activity does not necessarily have to be teacher-led. It still could involve child direction with an adult asking questions or providing support related to the standard. As the teacher reflects on how the children participated in the activity, she can ask herself the following questions:

- What steps of progress toward a particular early learning standard did the children show?
- If progress isn't apparent, did the children take the activity in a completely different direction?
- If so, was a different early learning standard addressed? Which one?

Even when teachers are intentional about early learning standards, there will always be some unintentional, naturally occurring results based on the individual performance of each child. Being intentional and yet being open to ways the children may change the plan requires great flexibility on the part of early educators. It also requires knowledge of standards from all domains so that standards other than the one planned for can be recognized.

We have found that planning a staff development activity where teachers play with open-ended materials helps them learn how standards can be seen naturally in children's play experiences. In Staff Development Activity 5, "Identifying Early Learning Standards in Self-Initiated Play," we have adapted workshops that have been presented by the NAEYC Play, Policy, and Practice Caucus. In our experience, the participants are often surprised by how much learning occurred as they played. These sessions can be a very powerful way for adults to see early learning standards in action through open-ended play. This type of activity is an example of the parallel process we spoke of in chapter 3: modeling developmentally appropriate practices with teachers.

Staff Development Activity 5

Identifying Early Learning Standards in Self-Initiated Play

Purpose: To provide teachers with a parallel process experience—playing with materials—and have them identify the early learning standards imbedded in that play.

What to Do: See PowerPoint slides 13 and 14.

This activity needs to be at least two hours long to provide for uninterrupted periods of play and debriefing. We use play kits containing recycled, open-ended materials. (You can put together kits yourself or purchase them from vendors such as Dr. Drew's Toys, Inc., P. O. 510501, Melbourne, FL 32951.) Set out the play kits in large plastic bags and allow the participants to choose what they want to play with. Play soft, soothing music during the play times.

Solo Play Experience: First, have the participants choose a material and play in silent, solo play for thirty minutes. After thirty minutes, have them document on paper what they used and what they did. Then have the solo players share their experience with another person.

Cooperative Play Experience: Next, have the participants engage in co-operative play, with two or more people playing together using two or more play kits. Again, this should go on for thirty minutes.

Group Discussion: After the thirty minutes of cooperative play, have the participants share in the large group the learning that occurred as they played. For example, they might note that they were using math skills as they compared the sizes of the materials or using cooperation as they played together to accomplish a goal. We recommend that you write their ideas on a flipchart. Then have the group look at your state's early learning standards and identify which ones encompass the learning that they identified for themselves.

• • • • • ◉ • • • • •

We believe that it is important for teachers to consider both ways of addressing standards in curriculum: naturally occurring activities and intentional activities. Staff Development Activity 6, "Analyzing Early Learning Standards and Generating Curricular Ideas," helps teachers do so. This activity makes use of charts developed to show curricular ideas related to early learning standards from across the U.S. (Gronlund 2006). You will see that these charts include a selected standard and identify three possible steps of progress a child might demonstrate toward accomplishing that standard. We will give a more in-depth explanation of ways to use these steps in chapter 7.

Staff Development Activity 6

Analyzing Early Learning Standards
and Generating Curricular Ideas

Purpose: To help teachers plan both naturalistic and intentional curricular activities directly tied to early learning standards.

What to Do: See PowerPoint slide 15. See handouts 4a and 4b.

Have the teachers analyze the chart of curricular ideas related to a standard in handout 4a. Although the chart may not be in reference to an early learning standard from your state, it can be used as a conversation starter to analyze your state's early learning standards and generate additional activities that could be used to facilitate children's progress toward those standards.

Group Discussion: Ask the following questions:

- Do the activity ideas listed on page 2 of handout 4a support the children's development of the skills or knowledge inherent in the standard identified?
- What additional activities would you do with children to address this standard?
- Do your state standards have any similarly worded expectations?

In handout 4b, we provide you with a blank chart. You can use this to have teachers identify curricular activity ideas that address a standard from your state.

• • • • • ◉ • • • •

Using Video Vignettes

We have found that video vignettes of children in action make excellent discussion starters. After watching a vignette, teachers can reflect and discuss, identifying what they saw the child doing, what questions arose as they watched, and what next steps they would take to help this child continue to grow and learn in that situation. The video *Focused Observations* (Gronlund and James 2005) contains 16 vignettes of toddlers and preschoolers in action. Many activities are outlined to guide the use of the vignettes in *Focused Observations: How to Observe Children for Assessment and Curriculum Planning* (Gronlund and James 2005). We have included several of these activities in this book and provided a selection of eight video vignettes on the DVD accompanying this book for you to use with these activities. To prepare for staff development activities, we suggest that you copy the PowerPoint file from the CD-ROM to your computer. Then, when you are ready to lead a group of teachers in an activity that uses a video vignette, you can show the PowerPoint slides using the file you saved to your computer, and then insert the DVD into your disc drive to show the vignettes.

Staff Development Activity 7, "Observation Practice: Encouraging and Extending a Child's Interests in an Intentional Curricular Activity," is an example of an activity that uses a video vignette. If you have the technological capability, we recommend that you film children in the classrooms of your program and use those vignettes instead, as they will be far more meaningful to the teachers.

Staff Development Activity 7

Observation Practice: Encouraging and Extending a Child's Interests in an Intentional Curricular Activity

Purpose: To determine ways to use materials to set up the environment and interact with a child to build on his interest.

What to Do: See PowerPoint slide 16.

Using the DVD accompanying this book, play vignette 1, "Tubes and Bottles," which shows Elias (2 years 1 month). Ask the participants to pay close attention to all of the things that Elias is able to do and is interested in; to focus on how the environment is set up with materials that interest him and ways that the teacher (whose voice is heard in the background) encourages his interest and learning.

Group Discussion: Ask the following questions:

- In what ways does the physical environment capture Elias's interests?
- In what ways does the teacher encourage him as he explores the bottles and the tubes and watches what is happening outside?
- What are some additional strategies to extend his interests and discoveries?

• • • • • ◉ • • • • •

Using Case Studies

Case studies can also be used in staff development sessions to help teachers reflect on curricular possibilities and the incorporation of early learning standards as well. As stated earlier, we give you a number of case studies in appendix B, where actual situations from preschool classrooms are described. You are welcome to use them. We also recommend that you invite teachers to share actual incidents from their own classrooms. They will gain the most value from those discussions.

Identifying Early Learning Standards in Play and Daily Routines

Not all teachers see the integration of early learning standards into play and daily routines as an easy process. We have used Staff Development Activity 8, "Identifying Early Learning Standards for Classroom Learning Areas," with a variety of teachers from across the country and have found it to be very beneficial and enlightening. It involves asking small groups of teachers to dialogue about the early learning standards that children could be showing in each of the learning areas of their classroom.

Staff Development Activity 8

*Identifying Early Learning Standards
for Classroom Learning Areas*

Purpose: To help teachers see that standards can be addressed as children play in various areas of the classroom.

What to Do: See PowerPoint slides 17 and 18. See handout 5.

Divide the large group into small teams of two to four teachers and either allow each group to choose a learning area or assign one to each group so that all learning areas are being addressed. Give each team a chart labeled with an area of a preschool classroom, such as Blocks, Dramatic Play, Art, Manipulatives, Sensory Table, Class Library, and Writing Center. Others, such as Science, Music, or Outdoors, can be included as well. We encourage teachers to expand the list to match the ways that they organize their classrooms. Have each team refer to your state's early learning standards documents and write on their chart the standards that children could be working on in that specific area of the classroom.

Group Discussion: Once a team has finished its chart, have the members post it on the wall for everyone to review. We recommend a "walkabout" as a way for all of the teams to view the standards identified for each of the classroom areas. Ask the members of each team to walk around and read each others' lists of standards. After all the participants have reviewed all of the charts, lead a discussion, asking the following questions:

- Was it difficult or easy to find standards that could be addressed in your group's learning area?

- Was there anything that surprised you as you did this activity?
- How will this impact your future planning for these learning areas?

You may want to make copies of these lists and give them to the members of the group to use as a reference when planning for children's engagement throughout their classrooms. In handout 5 we have provided a chart you can use to record the information generated from this activity so that teachers have an individual record of the standards they identified. This is an activity that you may wish to repeat periodically throughout the year to help teachers continue to see how standards can be integrated naturally in children's play and exploration.

• • • • • ⦿ • • • •

Creating Signs for Posting Standards

The Child and Family Development Center at San Juan College in Farmington, New Mexico, devised a way to keep a conversation going among its staff members about early learning standards and learning areas. Teachers made a sign for each learning area to which they affixed Velcro strips. The early learning standards from various domains were then printed in large print on cardstock, laminated, and affixed with the complementary Velcro strips.

The teachers display the signs in the appropriate classroom areas and regularly change the early learning standards listed on them. In this way, they are continually keeping in mind the correlation between children's play and learning. They also are paying attention to children's capabilities and interests and changing the early learning standards on the signs to reflect them.

These signs have been shared in staff development sessions across New Mexico and have been very well received by teachers, administrators, and parents alike. Teachers report that by changing the signs regularly, they continue to look for early learning standards occurring naturally as the children play and explore in the learning areas. The signs also remind them to think about intentionally addressing the goals written in their lesson plan. For example, a teacher may see a standard about measurement posted on the Block Area sign and remember to ask the children open-ended questions about the length of blocks or the height of towers. Administrators say that the signs help parents understand that during play the children are learning and that teachers are enhancing that learning in many ways. We recommend that you consider having a sign-making session with your teachers.

Standards and Daily Routines

In addition to identifying standards for each learning area, you can also have teachers identify standards that can be addressed in daily routines. Staff Development Activity 9, "Webbing Daily Routines and Early Learning Standards," gives guidelines and formats for such an activity.

Staff Development Activity 9

Webbing Daily Routines and Early Learning Standards

Purpose: To help teachers see that early learning standards are imbedded in the daily routines of classroom life.

What to Do: See PowerPoint slides 19–21. See handout 6.

Working in small groups of three or four, have the participants think about the daily routines in their classrooms (hand washing, toothbrushing, snack, arrival and departure, toileting). Then, using handout 6, ask them to create webs identifying one early learning standard for each domain that could be addressed as children participate in that daily routine. The format for the web is shown on handout 6.

Group Discussion: When the participants have completed the handout 6 webs, have them share the standards they identified in each domain. Ask the following questions as this sharing goes on:

- Did you realize that standards could be imbedded in daily routines?
- Were you surprised at how many could be addressed?
- How will you help yourself to remember to address standards at these times of the day?

Again, we recommend that this be not just a one-time-only activity. You will want to revisit the importance of enhancing routines as a part of curriculum.

• • • • • ◉ • • • • •

Planning for Integration of Early Learning Standards

Documenting attention to standards in lesson or activity plans is another step in integrating early learning standards. The Focused Early Learning Planning and Reflection Frameworks, created by Gaye Gronlund (2003), are set up in such a way that teachers are being intentional not only for teacher-led activities, but also for the child-initiated ones. Using the Focused Early Learning Weekly Planning Framework, teachers can write goals based on early learning standards for each of the areas in the classroom and for teacher-led small and large groups. The identification of goals helps them provide materials and experiences for children's exploration and play that relate to that goal. For example, a teacher may identify the following goal for the sensory table: "Children will use their senses to explore the physical and natural world." To meet that goal she will provide materials such as water, sand, or shaving cream for the children's exploration. The children's actions will still be natural and self-initiated and the teacher will interact with them in ways that encourage their sensory exploration and develop their vocabulary as to the properties and characteristics of the substance they are using.

You will want to remind teachers that reflection is also a part of the planning process. Teachers reflect and evaluate how well activities went and in what directions the children took them. The Focused Early Learning General Reflection Framework provides a format for teachers to think about what children did with materials and to identify their learning, as well as to evaluate the success of the activity. This reflection process becomes critical to ongoing assessment of children's performance as well as to future planning. An important part of the reflection process is determining if and when it is appropriate to change materials and goals. "[G]oals could continue for several weeks. The selection of materials in each area should be extensive and rich enough so the children will continue to explore the possibilities for using those materials. . . . The following circumstances, however, warrant change:

- The children are ignoring a particular area.
- The children are bored with what's available.

- The children's behavior is not productive or positive in an area.
- The materials could be changed to support an interest of the children, a developmental need, a topic of study, or a project that has emerged in the classroom" (Gronlund 2003, 28–29).

In Staff Development Activity 10, "Using Planning and Reflection Frameworks," we give you the Focused Early Learning Weekly Planning Framework and the Focused Early Learning General Reflection Framework to try out with teachers.

Staff Development Activity 10

Using Planning and Reflection Frameworks

Purpose: To provide teachers with ways to write out plans that address goals and/or standards as well as to document the end results of such plans.

What to Do: See PowerPoint slides 22 and 23. See handouts 7a and 7b.

Have the participants look through the Focused Early Learning Weekly Planning Framework (handout 7a) and identify possible goals for each of the learning areas, for the academic sections, for physical energy outlets and outdoor play, and for small and large group times. Point out the other sections of the framework and discuss ways that individual adjustments can be made as well as steps that teachers can take to build relationships with children. Let the participants know that the focused observations portion can be used to document which children or standards will be observed.

Then review the Focused Early Learning General Reflection Framework (handout 7b). Ask participants to consider a recent week with their children and fill out the framework in ways that shows what happened in their classrooms.

Group Discussion: Ask the following questions as the discussion ensues:

- How might you use this framework or another lesson planning format to show how you are addressing goals and standards with the children?
- In what ways do you use reflection now to consider what children did with specific activities and how that might impact future planning?

· · · · · ◉ · · · · ·

Analyzing Lesson Plans

No matter what lesson plan format is used by teachers, attention to goals and standards should be evident throughout the plan, not just in teacher-led activities. In Staff Development Activity 11, "Analyzing Lesson Plans," four examples of lesson plans are given in a variety of formats for teachers to review. Suggested criteria for that analysis are also included.

Staff Development Activity 11

Analyzing Lesson Plans

Purpose: To help teachers consider ways to address goals and/or standards as well as levels of child engagement in lesson planning.

What to Do: See PowerPoint slides 24 and 25. See handout 8.

This activity is most effective when teachers analyze their own lesson plans. However, it may be best to begin by analyzing some examples in order to get the conversation started and to establish a climate of sharing and trust. Either individually or in teams of two or three, have the participants look over the selection of lesson plans provided in handout 8. Ask them to evaluate the plans based on the following criteria:

1. Does the lesson plan reflect clear learning goals for most or all of the activities (not just the teacher-led ones)?
2. Are the goals age-appropriate and broad enough to account for individual differences among the children?
3. Do the goals extend across many developmental domains or areas (for example, some language goals, some social/emotional goals, some fine motor goals, some cognitive goals, and so on)?
4. Is there a balance between child-initiated and teacher-led activities or are the activities more heavily weighted toward the child-initiated ones?
5. Do you think the activities identified will be interesting and engaging to the children?

6. Are learning areas identified and planned for (for example, blocks, dramatic play, art, sensory table, and so on)?
7. Are there plans for small group activities and do they look like they are rich enough to keep the children's interest for up to fifteen minutes at a time?
8. Are there plans for large group activities and do they include movement and music, as well as story reading and teacher presentations?

Group Discussion: Go through each of the plans as a large group, using the questions above to guide the discussion. Encourage teachers to consider ways that they incorporate goals and standards into their lesson planning process, as well as to share ways that they pay attention to children's engagement levels and other factors as identified above.

• • • • • ⦿ • • • • •

Relating Projects to Early Learning Standards

We find it helpful to remind teachers that when they are planning projects or studies of interest to the children, they can relate the activities to early learning standards. One of the lesson plans from handout 8 in Staff Development Activity 11 shows activities and goals around the topic of "harvest." You can use that plan as a basis for discussion or have teachers look at their own plans related to topics or themes and identify the standards that are being addressed. Staff Development Activity 12, "Projects, Studies, and Standards," gives suggestions for such an activity.

Staff Development Activity 12
. . . .
Projects, Studies, and Standards

Purpose: To help teachers see that standards can be addressed through in-depth projects and studies.

What to Do: See PowerPoint slides 26 and 27.

Ask teachers to bring their lesson plans, reflections, and documentation for an in-depth project, exploration, study, or set of thematic activities that they have implemented with the children. We suggest that it be a project that was done in the past so that they have documentation to review. Using copies of your state's early learning standards documents, have the participants individually or in teams of two or three, identify the standards that were addressed in the activities.

Encourage teachers to review the documentation of children's investigations related to this topic. Then ask them to label the photos and work samples with the standards that were imbedded in the work the children were doing.

Group Discussion: First, invite individuals or teams to share with the large group the standards that they addressed in their projects and thematic activities. Validate whichever ones they identify and invite contributions from others for additional possibilities. Then do a "walk about" so the participants can look at each other's documentation with the standards labels added. Again, celebrate and validate the learning that is identified and invite additional suggestions for possible standards addressed. After reviewing the documentation, use the following questions to guide a large group discussion.

- Were you surprised at how many standards were being addressed in your projects?
- Was it easy or hard to figure out which ones were included?
- How do you think this will help parents and family members to better understand your curriculum planning for the children?
- How else will you relate standards and goals to your documentation photos and work samples?

• • • • • ◉ • • • • •

In the next chapter, we will discuss the best ways to assess young children's performance in relation to early learning standards. Again, we will provide staff development activities as well as coaching strategies to help teachers make changes in their assessment practices.

References

Gronlund, Gaye. 2003. *Focused early learning: A planning framework for teaching young children.* St. Paul: Redleaf Press.

Gronlund, Gaye. 2006. *Make early learning standards come alive: Connecting your practice and curriculum to state guidelines.* St. Paul: Redleaf Press.

Gronlund, Gaye, and Marlyn James. 2005. *Focused observations: How to observe children for curriculum and assessment.* St. Paul: Redleaf Press.

Helping Others Implement Assessment Practices in Ways Best for Young Children

As stated in the previous chapter, assessment is interwoven with curriculum. The two cannot be separated. In fact, it's been our experience that assessment *drives* curriculum. If teachers are asked to test children inappropriately through on-demand, one-shot tasks, they tend to see curriculum as more teacher-directed, and start to focus on working on the tasks that will be tested. In contrast, if teachers are asked to use authentic assessment processes based on observation of children in action, they tend to see curriculum encompassing more than just teacher-led activities. We have seen that as teachers become more comfortable with observing for assessment purposes, they change their thinking about curriculum. They begin to recognize the potential for children's learning to occur throughout the day, not just in large or small group times. They allow themselves to interact with children in other roles besides instructor. They are much more aware of the value of child-directed play and exploration, and figure out ways to support it. Therefore, we believe strongly that to help others implement assessment and curriculum that are best for young children, we must focus on authentic assessment procedures and enable teachers to become effective observers and documenters.

In this chapter, we will look at the many aspects of assessment and provide five staff development activities (numbered 13 through 17) that address the following:

- clarifying the purposes of developmental screening instruments and observational assessment methods
- writing objective and factual documentation
- using different formats for documentation

As we did in chapters 4 and 5, for each of the staff development activities, we will reference PowerPoint slides. For some of the activities, we will also provide handouts or case studies, or refer to video vignettes that you can use. The handouts and case studies can be found in appendixes A and B, respectively, as well as on the CD accompanying this book. You will want to make your copies from the CD. The PowerPoint slides are also on the CD. The video vignettes can be found on the accompanying DVD.

In chapter 8, we will look at various forms of resistance that teachers may demonstrate as they attempt to make changes in assessment related to the points above. We will offer coaching strategies to help you address these forms of resistance and help teachers embrace new ideas about assessment for young children.

Types of Assessment

We will focus on two types of assessment: developmental screening and observational assessment. You will notice that we are not recommending the use of any form of standardized testing. The following quote comes from a joint position statement from NAEYC and the National Association of Early Childhood Specialists in State Departments of Education (2003, 10) and encourages looking beyond standardized testing to other types of assessment:

> Often people think of assessment as formal testing only, but assessment has many components and many purposes. Assessment methods include observation, documentation of children's work, checklists and rating scales, and portfolios, as well as norm-referenced tests. . . .
>
> High-quality programs are "informed by ongoing systematic, formal, and informal assessment approaches to provide information on children's learning and development. These assessments occur within the context of reciprocal communications with families and with sensitivity to the cultural contexts in which children develop" (Commission on NAEYC Early Childhood Program Standards and Accreditation Criteria 2003, np).
>
> . . . In general, assessment specialists have urged great caution in the use and interpretation of standardized tests of young children's learning, especially in the absence of complementary evidence when the stakes are potentially high (National Research Council 1999; Jones 2003; Scott-Little, Kagan, and Clifford 2003).

Our primary focus in this chapter will be to provide ways to help teachers implement observational assessment and use the information gained to help them teach children more effectively. We know that teachers watch their children all the time. They take in information and make multiple decisions about how to best help each child grow and learn. When this "child watching" is used as the source for assessment of children's progress, it moves from being an informal process to a more formal one. In your work as a staff development specialist, you can provide support for teachers to be more systematic in their observations and to choose the documentation formats that best show what children can do. The Council for Chief State School Officers Early Childhood Education Assessment Panel (2003) defines observational assessment as:

> A process in which the teacher systematically observes and records information about the child's level of development and/or knowledge, skills, and attitudes in order to determine what has been learned, improve teaching, and support the child's progress. A checklist or notes are often used to record what has been observed. Effective observational assessment involves recording children's behavior at the time it occurs and training observers to be objective in recording behavioral descriptions. Many early childhood educators believe that observational assessment is the most valid form of assessment for use with young children because of their limitations to show what they know through conventional pencil-and-paper tests.

Also, the NAEYC assessment criteria identified in the accreditation standards emphasize the importance of observation: "Teachers observe and document children's work, play, behaviors, and interactions to assess progress. They use the information gathered to plan and modify the curriculum and their teaching" (NAEYC 2005, 37). This type of observational assessment is ongoing and is used to improve instruction and individualize curriculum.

Developmental Screening

Developmental screening is another type of assessment that is addressed in the NAEYC accreditation criteria. The purpose of developmental screening is to provide a first look at a child. The criteria state that a developmental screening instrument is to be administered to each child within three months of enrollment (NAEYC 2005, 36). This is identified as an emerging practice. Therefore, it is important to familiarize teachers with the assessment processes involved in developmental screening.

> It serves as the first step in a prevention, evaluation, and intervention process that is intended to help children achieve their potential. . . . Developmental screening tests (or "instruments") briefly survey a young child's abilities in language, reasoning, gross motor, fine motor, and personal social development to determine quickly and efficiently whether

*that child should undergo further assessment and evaluation. . . . In ad-
dition to developmental screening instruments, information about children should be collected from medical examinations, hearing and vision
tests, and parent questionnaires and interviews (Meisels and Atkins-
Burnett 2005, 5–6).*

The developmental screening process differs from more in-depth observational
assessment in that it is not meant to provide detailed information about a
child's progress in attaining skills or concepts, nor for curricular planning. The
purpose of developmental screening is to identify learning and/or behavioral
problems in a quick and easy way. In addition, the NAEYC accreditation
standards state that the "screening instrument . . . meets professional standards
for standardization, reliability, and validity" (NAEYC 2005, 36). Therefore,
using appropriate instruments is critical.

Most screening instruments are administered by an adult in a one-on-one
situation with a child. And yet, observation still plays a key part in the process.
"In addition to the standardized information provided by the developmental
screening instrument, a great deal of observational data about the child can be
gained from screening" (Meisels and Atkins-Burnett 2005, 10). It is possible to
use some screening instruments as you observe children participating in daily
activities and routines. Staff Development Activity 13, "Using Observation and
Documentation in Administering Developmental Screening Instruments,"
gives ideas for helping teachers determine which components of a screening
instrument can be accomplished while observing children's self-directed play
or participation in activities.

Staff Development Activity 13

*Using Observation and Documentation in Administering
Developmental Screening Instruments*

Purpose: To have teachers explore relating observations to a developmental
screening instrument.

What to Do: See PowerPoint slides 28 and 29.

Ask your teachers to bring some of their written observations of children
in action to this session. Then, in small groups, have them compare their
documentation with the criteria of a developmental screening tool. (We have
used the Ages & Stages Questionnaires in our trainings.) Ask each group to
generate a list of examples from the screening tool that they had written about

in their observation notes. Ask each group to write their list on a chart and post it for others to see.

Group Discussion: Follow with large group discussion using the following questions:

- Were you able to find most of the screening criteria in your observations?
- Were there some things that you were not able to find?
- Do you think that there are some things that would have to be assessed one-on-one with a child or in conversation with family members?
- Can most of the criteria be observed through children's self-initiated play, or are there some criteria that you would be able to observe by setting up an activity for the children to do during their play?
- Did the screening procedure help you to pick up on any potential problems?

This activity can be a way for teachers not only to see the benefits of early screening but also to understand how much of the criteria they may be able to observe in their daily practices with children.

• • • • • ⦿ • • • • •

Ongoing Observational Assessment

To help teachers more fully understand ongoing observational assessment, we recommend that you emphasize the following key characteristics:

- Observational assessment is ongoing and imbedded in the daily curriculum.
- The written documentation should be objective and factual and can be done in many different formats.
- It is criterion-based—the child's capabilities are evaluated in relation to clearly identified standards, not in comparison to the performance of other children.
- It is individualized so that the documentation creates a full and rich picture of each child's strengths, learning styles, and interests.
- It is used to improve teaching.

Many staff development activities can address these key characteristics and help teachers learn to sharpen their observation skills and improve their written documentation, as well as become more efficient in their organization and time management regarding observational assessment.

We feel that it is important to help teachers see that assessment of children's capabilities and progress toward standards can be done in everyday activities. Video vignettes or actual classroom observations can be used to illustrate this point. The vignette that is recommended in Staff Development Activity 14, "Observing a Child at Snack Time," is one that we have used many times with great success. We invite you to use it as is or adapt the suggested activity to a video vignette or a written classroom observation from your own program.

Staff Development Activity 14

Observing a Child at Snack Time

Purpose: To identify what can be learned by observing a child engaged in a daily routine.

What to Do: See PowerPoint slides 30 and 31.

Using the DVD accompanying this book, play vignette 2, "Washing Hands and Snack," which shows Daniel (4 years 2 months) as he goes through the daily routine of snack time. As teachers watch, ask them to make notes about all the things they see that Daniel can do.

Group Discussion: As the group shares what they observed, generate a list of what they learned about Daniel's capabilities, skills, social interactions, personality traits, and behaviors, and discuss these questions:

- Were you surprised at how much you learned in a short observation?
- If you had a history with Daniel, do you think that you would have seen things differently? If so, in what ways?
- What curriculum plans might you make for Daniel based on what you learned about him?

You can also have the participants relate their observations of what Daniel could do to your state's early learning standards. This becomes a powerful way to illustrate how children's progress toward standards can be observed in everyday activities, not just in teacher-led instruction.

Writing Objective and Factual Documentation

Writing an objective, factual description of what a child did and/or said takes practice and focused attention. It also lends much more credibility to documentation, so that it serves as evidence of what the child can do, not as a representation of the teacher's opinion or judgment of the child's capabilities. In order to stimulate teachers' thinking about factual documentation we have them read through observational anecdotes and analyze them for factual versus interpretive language. We use the following chart of words and phrases as a reference.

Words and Phrases to Avoid	Words and Phrases to Use
• The child loves . . .	• He often chooses . . .
• The child likes . . .	• I saw him . . .
• He enjoys . . .	• I heard her say . . .
• She spends a long time at . . .	• He spends five minutes doing . . .
• It seems like . . .	• She said . . .
• It appears . . .	• Almost every day he . . .
• I thought . . .	• Once or twice a month, she . . .
• I felt . . .	• Each time, he . . .
• I wonder . . .	• She consistently . . .
• He does . . . very well . . .	• We observed a pattern of . . .
• She is bad at . . .	
• This is difficult for . . .	

Staff Development Activity 15, "Factual vs. Interpretive Documentation," includes several anecdotes to analyze using the chart above.

Staff Development Activity 15
. . . .
Factual vs. Interpretive Documentation

Purpose: To give teachers an opportunity to analyze the language in observational documentation and distinguish between words and phrases that are factual and descriptive and those that are interpretive or judgmental.

What to Do: See PowerPoint slides 32–35. See handouts 9a and 9b.

Using the chart of words and phrases in handout 9a, have the group analyze the following anecdotes, taken from *Focused Observations* (Gronlund and James 2005), identifying words and phrases that are interpretive or judgmental in nature. The anecdotes are provided on handout 9b. Then ask them to edit and replace those words and phrases with ones that are factual, descriptive, and objective. For your reference, we have identified the interpretive words and made suggestions for edits that would make these observation notes more objective. Handout 9b includes only the interpretive anecdotes so that the participants can try this on their own.

Jennifer (6 months)

Jennifer is a very fussy baby. She cries when her mom leaves. She demands a lot of adult attention. She has trouble settling down unless she has her pacifier or is being held. She startles easily and gets upset when other toddlers come near her.

Interpretive words: "very fussy," "demands," "has trouble," and "gets upset."

Possible rewrite with editing: "Jennifer cries often. She settles down when she has her pacifier or is being held. She startles easily and may cry when other toddlers come near her."

Carrie (3 years 2 months)

Carrie runs outside to the bikes at riding time because she wants to have first choice of the bikes. She always wants the red bike and forgets the rule of walking outside to the bike area.

Interpretive words: "she wants," "always wants," and "forgets the rule."

Possible rewrite with editing: "Carrie runs outside to the bikes at riding time almost every day. She announces, 'I want the red bike,' but will ride other colors if that one is not available."

> ## Max (2 years 6 months)
>
> During art time today, Max really enjoyed painting a picture. He used up a lot of paint—green, blue, brown, and red. His picture is very interesting. It looks like he painted some people and a house. Max paints almost every day, and it seems to be his favorite activity."
>
> *Interpretive words:* "really enjoyed," "very interesting," "looks like," and "seems."
>
> *Possible rewrite with editing:* "During art time today, Max painted a picture using lots of paint and colors. I asked him what he painted and he replied, 'Some people and a house.' He paints almost every day and stays engaged for up to fifteen minutes doing so."

Group Discussion: As you lead a discussion about the language in these anecdotes, assure the group that writing factually and objectively takes conscious effort and careful thinking about the words and phrases to best describe what a child does. It is easy for a teacher to quickly move into judgment and evaluation. It's okay to do so in one's mind in order to figure out the best ways to support a child, but it is not okay to write judgments and evaluations in the documentation.

You can also invite teachers to review their own written observations using the chart and edit their own documentation. We have found that it's helpful to print the chart on card stock and laminate it so that it is available as a reference whenever teachers are writing anecdotes.

• • • • • ◉ • • • • •

Gathering Evidence for Accurate Evaluation

We recognize that it is also important to help teachers understand that assessment is a process of both documentation *and* evaluation. The goal is to have factual evidence (the objective observation note) to support the conclusions made in the evaluation process. One does not want to jump to evaluation too quickly and possibly draw an inaccurate conclusion about a child's capabilities. You will want to emphasize the necessity of collecting enough evidence through written notes to support a conclusion that is as valid as possible. Staff Development Activity 16, "Interpreting Children's Actions," can help to make this point.

Staff Development Activity 16

Interpreting Children's Actions

Purpose: To help teachers see that many different interpretations can be made regarding a child's actions.

What to Do: See PowerPoint slides 36 and 37. See handout 10.

Ask your teachers to read the following description of Elijah in the block area (also on handout 10). The description is taken from *Focused Observations* (Gronlund and James 2005).

> ## Elijah (3 years 9 months)
>
> Elijah is in the block area. He has several animals in his hand. Several other children are in this area with him. He runs around in circles with the animals, and another child chases him. He laughs and screams, "You can't catch me!"

Group Discussion: Ask the group to identify as many different conclusions about Elijah's actions as they can. We suggest that you label a chart with the words "Possible Interpretations" and then write down the ideas generated by the group. As you write each one, put a question mark after it. This will help make the point that the only way a teacher will know if her conclusion is true for Elijah will be to watch him again and see if he does something similar or not. Possible interpretations may include:

He's a very active, noisy child.
He was attempting to get the other children to play with him.
The class had just read "The Gingerbread Boy" and he was acting it out.
He and his friends had made up a game of chase with the animals.

Lead a discussion about possible teacher interventions, depending on which of the interpretations are accurate. For example, if Elijah is acting out "The Gingerbread Boy," what could a teacher do to extend that play? How would the teacher's intervention change if Elijah is attempting to get others to play?

• • • • • ◉ • • • • •

Different Formats for Documentation

We find that it is important to remind teachers that there are many formats for documenting observations. A teacher determines which format is right for her depending on the situation, the number of children, the goal of the activity, and her own organizational style. Using video clips is one way to have teachers practice a variety of methods. Staff Development Activity 17, "Using Summative Anecdotes," involves teachers in viewing a video clip and writing a summary of what the child did. In the next chapter, we show other documentation formats as well.

Staff Development Activity 17

Using Summative Anecdotes

Purpose: To provide teachers with an opportunity to practice writing an observation note that summarizes what they have seen a child do.

What to Do: See PowerPoint slides 38 and 39.

Using the DVD accompanying this book, play vignette 3, "Painting," which shows Megan (4 years 8 months). Ask the teachers to pay close attention to what Megan does, but hold off writing down their observations while they are watching. Instead, after the vignette is over, they may write down two to four sentences summarizing what they saw Megan do. Remind them to be factual and descriptive, not interpretive, in their choice of words and phrases.

Group Discussion: Share some of the summative anecdotes recorded by the group. Discuss the ease or difficulty of trying this type of documentation. Ask the following questions:

- Could this type of documentation be done while you were in the middle of running a busy classroom?
- How practical is such a recording method for your setting?

There are many ways to help teachers sharpen their observation skills and improve their written documentation of what they have seen children do. More tips and strategies for doing so are outlined in our book, *Focused Observations: How to Observe Children for Assessment and Curriculum Planning* (Gronlund and James 2005). In the next chapter, we provide an additional seven staff development activities to help teachers relate their observations to early learning standards.

References

Bricker, Diane, and Jane Squires. 1999. Ages & stages questionnaires (ASQ): A parent-completed, child-monitoring system. 2nd ed. Baltimore, Md.: Brooks Publishing Co.

Commission on NAEYC Early Childhood Program Standards and Accreditation Criteria. 2003. Draft NAEYC early childhood program standards. Accessed July 9, 2007, at www.naeyc.org/accreditation/nextera.asp.

Council for Chief State School Officers Early Childhood Education Assessment Panel. 2003. The words we use: A glossary of terms for early childhood education standards and assessment. Accessed June 4, 2007, at www.ccsso.org.

Gronlund, Gaye, and Marlyn James. 2005. *Focused observations: How to observe children for assessment and curriculum planning.* St. Paul: Redleaf Press.

Jones, J. 2003. *Early literacy assessment systems: Essential elements.* Princeton, N.J.: Educational Testing Service.

Meisels, Samuel J., and Sally Atkins-Burnett. 2005. *Developmental screening in early childhood: A guide,* 5th ed. Washington, D.C.: National Association for the Education of Young Children.

NAEYC. 2005. *Early childhood program standards and accreditation criteria.* Washington, D.C.: National Association for the Education of Young Children.

National Association for the Education of Young Children and the National Association of Early Childhood Specialists in State Departments of Education. 2003. Early childhood curriculum, assessment, and program evaluation: Building an effective, accountable system in programs for children birth through age 8. Accessed June 3, 2007, at www.naeyc.org/about/positions/pdf/CAPEexpand.pdf, page 10.

National Research Council. 1999. High stakes: Testing for tracking, promotion, and graduation. Committee on Appropriate Test Use, eds. J. P. Heubert and R. M. Hauser. Washington, D.C.: National Academy Press.

Scott-Little, C., S. L. Kagan, and R. M. Clifford, eds. 2003. *Assessing the state of state assessment: Perspectives on assessing young children.* Greensboro, N.C.: SERVE.

Evaluating Observations Related to Early Learning Standards

Early learning standards become the reference by which teachers evaluate their observations. The accountability to these standards gives teachers a firm foundation on which to base their evaluations of children's performance and progress. They are not just relying on their own knowledge of child development. They are using a clear set of criteria that has been developed by early educators in their state.

In this chapter we provide an additional seven staff development activities (numbered 18 through 24) that address the following:

- imbedding observational assessment related to early learning standards in everyday classroom activities
- evaluating observations related to early learning standards
- documenting children's steps of progress in both quick and easy ways and in more in-depth portfolio collections
- assessing what children can do, rather than what they cannot
- building a case about each child across several domains
- using observational assessment to improve teaching

As we did in earlier chapters, we will reference PowerPoint slides for each staff development activity. For some of the activities, we will provide handouts or case studies or refer to video vignettes that you can use. The handouts and case studies can be found in appendixes A and B, respectively, as well as on the CD accompanying the book. You will want to make your copies from the CD. The PowerPoint slides are also on the CD. The video vignettes can be found on the accompanying DVD.

In chapter 8, we will look at various forms of resistance that teachers may demonstrate as they attempt to make changes in assessment related to the points above. We will offer coaching strategies to help you address these forms of resistance and help teachers embrace new ideas about assessment for young children.

We have found that by practicing observing a child in action and evaluating his progress toward specific standards, teachers get better acquainted with their state's expectations. You can help them in this familiarization process by asking them to analyze video clips as well as observation notes.

Identifying Developmental Skills

Staff Development Activity 18, "Identifying Developmental Areas and Specific Skills," is an example of an activity using an observation note to evaluate a child's capabilities and skills.

Staff Development Activity 18

Identifying Developmental Areas and Specific Skills

Purpose: To analyze observation notes and determine what developmental skills the child is demonstrating.

What to Do: See PowerPoint slides 40 and 41. See handout 11.

Have your teachers read the following anecdote (also on handout 11) about JoAnngela (3 years 8 months). The anecdote is taken from *Focused Observations* (Gronlund and James 2005).

> JoAnngela, Damien, and Adrianne sit down with me to read "The Three Little Pigs." JoAnngela sits for a while listening to the story. About halfway through the story, she gets on her knees and begins to rock back and forth. She bumps into Damien and tells him, "Sorry, Damien." She then stands up, moves to the other side of Adrianne, curls up on the beanbag, and finishes listening to the story.

Ask the teachers to analyze the observation and identify the evidence that they see to support conclusions about JoAnngela's capabilities in the areas of cognitive, social, emotional, and physical development.

Group Discussion: Then, as a group, review your state's early learning standards and evaluate JoAnngela's progress toward accomplishing some of those standards. You may want to divide the group into teams of two or three people and ask each team to look up the standards in a specific domain. Then have each team report back to the group on the standards that they could see JoAnngela demonstrating in the observation.

This same activity can be done with other anecdotes or by watching video clips of children in action. In appendix B, we give you several more anecdotes to use for such activities. Again, we strongly recommend that you also use written observations from the teachers' classrooms. Having the opportunity to analyze observations of the children with whom they work every day will be far more powerful and meaningful for teachers.

• • • • • ◉ • • • • •

Assessing Children's Progress toward Standards

We believe that it is important to emphasize that most children are making some steps toward accomplishing a standard, even though they may not be at a predetermined proficiency level. When evaluating children's progress, we recommend that a set of rubrics be developed to capture smaller steps the child is making toward accomplishing the standard:

> *Not all children will accomplish every early learning standard. Instead, they will show variability in their capabilities with strengths in some areas and weaknesses in others. If only two ratings were included, such as Accomplished and Not Accomplished, small steps toward an early learning standard would be completely lost and many children would appear to be failing. In using three or four ratings, early educators can identify more clearly just where the child stands in relation to the expectation. This will help with planning curriculum for that child and give a more accurate picture of the child's progress than a simple "Yes" or "No" related to a standard (Gronlund 2006, 21).*

As we showed in chapter 5, you can identify three steps to measure a child's progress toward accomplishing a standard, such as:

1. First steps toward the standard
2. Making progress toward the standard
3. Accomplishing the standard

In her book *Make Early Learning Standards Come Alive*, Gaye Gronlund provides charts with examples of children's performance at each of these levels in relation to a selection of early learning standards from across the nation. By reviewing the charts, teachers can consider ways that a child might demonstrate her progress toward a standard. In Staff Development Activity 6 we suggested that you use these charts with your teachers to consider curricular planning with standards in mind.

In her work with the State of New Mexico PreK Program, Gronlund and her colleagues adapted this model and identified three performance steps related to each of the New Mexico PreK Essential Indicators based on the New Mexico PreK Early Learning Outcomes. Here is an example:

> *Early Learning Indicator: Adapts behavior to fit different situations (for example, accepts transitions, follows daily routines and/or incorporates cultural expectations).*
> *First Steps: Adapts behavior in one situation or adapts behavior only once in a while.*
> *Making Progress toward the Outcome: Adapts behavior in more than one situation and on a more regular basis.*
> *Accomplishing the Outcome: Adapts behavior frequently in a variety of situations.*

In staff development sessions with hundreds of teachers across the state, Gronlund and her colleagues have used video vignettes to help teachers observe children in action and rate children's progress toward these learning outcomes. Rich discussions have ensued, with teachers learning to make evaluations based on the performance of the child, not on intuitive feelings, guesses, or unsubstantiated judgments. Marlyn James has found this to work well with college students using the standards of her state as well.

Whether or not your state has identified steps of progress such as these, you can lead staff development activities in which teachers evaluate children's performance using a scale of this sort. You may use the charts from *Make Early Learning Standards Come Alive* and adapt them to reflect your state's early learning standards. Or you may work with teachers to identify three or four steps of progress for your state's early learning standards. Staff Development Activity 19, "Identifying Steps of Progress," uses one of Gronlund's charts.

Staff Development Activity 19

Identifying Steps of Progress

Purpose: To give teachers practice in looking at children's progress toward standards in smaller steps.

What to Do: See PowerPoint slides 42 and 43. See handout 12.

Using the DVD accompanying this book, play vignette 4, "Three Young Writers," which shows Tyler (4 years 4 months), Malik (4 years 5 months), and Dontasia (4 years 1 month). Have the participants watch the video and evaluate each child's performance related to the specific standard as shown on the chart in handout 12. Ask them to rate the child at one of the three levels of progress. If a participant feels that a child is between two of the levels, the rating should go to the lower of the two, as the child has not demonstrated the capability to be rated at the higher one.

Group Discussion: After the participants have identified a level for each child's performance, lead a group discussion about how they came to their conclusions. Ask the following questions:

- What did you see each of the children do that led you to your rating?
- Was it difficult to figure out your ratings? What factors did you have to take into consideration?

If you have some disagreement among the group, encourage the teachers to share their reasons for their choices. Total agreement in ratings is not necessary. Good discussion and critical thinking about children's performance is most important.

We recommend that you look through other charts in *Make Early Learning Standards Come Alive* and find any pages that reflect your state's early learning standards. If there are any, you can use them for a similar activity. Use video vignettes or observation notes about children in your program and have participants evaluate their performance related to specific standards on three or four points of progress.

Documenting Children's Steps of Progress

It is important to note that some early learning standards can be assessed quickly and easily based on a one-time observation and that formats can be developed for quick and easy documentation. The critical component is that the teacher observes to see how each child demonstrates what he can do in his own unique way.

Other standards cannot be assessed based on a quick, one-time observation because they are deeper and/or broader in scope. The richness of the child's progress toward these standards is best reflected in a portfolio collection of more in-depth observations that may be accompanied by work samples or photographs of the child in action. Identifying the best way to document a standard is an important step in order to help teachers assess children's performance in time-efficient and manageable ways. Barbara Bowman (2006, 47) suggests that teachers use standards judiciously, "thinking carefully about assessing different learning at different times and in different ways. For example, teachers spend hours writing anecdotal notes on skills that could be readily assessed in a monthly activity and a checklist, saving teacher time for those standards that do not lend themselves to quick and easy assessment."

Standards that fit into the quick-and-easy documentation mode generally can be reflected in a yes or no answer to the question, "Does this child do this skill or demonstrate understanding of this concept?" Here are some examples of early learning standards that lend themselves to a quick observation.

> *Wyoming Early Childhood Readiness Standards, Gross Motor: "The child demonstrates control, balance, strength and coordination in gross motor tasks" (Gronlund 2006, 108).*

> *Colorado Building Blocks, Science Standard: "Uses tools to gather information (e.g., magnifying lens, eyedropper, audiocassettes)" (Gronlund 2006, 68).*

For the New Mexico PreK Programs, Gronlund and colleagues designed an adaptation of the Quick Check Recording Sheet found in *Focused Observations* (Gronlund and James 2005). Listed on this sheet are some of the New Mexico PreK Essential Indicators that can be documented quickly. In addition, brief language describing the three rubric ratings is included so that teachers can quickly write down "1," "2," or "3" as they observe children. Even though this is for quick documentation purposes, teachers are strongly encouraged to watch children across time, in multiple situations, rather than observing everyone on one day and/or everyone in the same exact activity.

Quick Check Recording Sheet: New Mexico PreK

Children's Names	Date & Activity EI #1 Body coordination	Date & Activity EI #2 Eye-hand coordination	Date & Activity EI #3 Increasingly follows rules	Date & Activity EI #10 Concepts of print
First steps (#1)	1–2 movements	With larger items	Only when reminded	Awareness of ABC's
Making progress (#2)	3–4 movements	Smaller with help	Follows some	First letter of name
Accomplished (#3)	4+ movements	Variety of small items	Follows most	Some letters

Teachers have reported that this form of documentation is a timesaver. They say that it gives them time to focus intently on the standards that require a more in-depth set of observations to assess the child's progress. For these standards, a portfolio collection of written documentation with photos and/or work samples is necessary to provide evidence of a child's progress. Here are some examples of such standards.

> *Vermont Early Learning Standards: "Children show interest and curiosity in counting and grouping objects and numbers" (Gronlund 2006, 48).*

There are so many different ways that children show their interest and curiosity in counting and numbers that this standard is best documented in a description of what each individual child does. For example, one child might count the number of children when lining up; another, the number of crackers served at snack time or the number of specific materials being used in learning areas. Or a teacher may help a child count the number of children present or the days of the week.

> *California Desired Results: "Uses pretend writing during play activities (e.g., scribbles lines and shapes)" (Gronlund 2006, 40).*

This standard is best documented with samples of the child's writing accompanied by a description of the context in which they were produced. Was the child writing a grocery list, a list of their friends' names, or a letter to Grandma? This information and the accompanying work sample will support the evaluation of the child's progress level.

Staff Development Activity 20, "Quick and Easy or In-Depth Documentation?" asks teachers to analyze early learning standards and identify the best documentation strategy. We have found that this process helps teachers address time issues regarding assessment, as well as gain more knowledge of the standards themselves.

Staff Development Activity 20

Quick and Easy or In-Depth Documentation?

Purpose: To determine the best documentation format for different early learning standards.

What to Do: See PowerPoint slides 44 and 45. See handout 13.

Have the participants analyze your state's early learning standards and identify which ones fit in the quick-and-easy category of documentation versus those that require more in-depth attention. Use the following criteria:

- Is this a standard that can be assessed by asking a yes or no question?
- Or is this a standard that requires in-depth observation and involvement, and that will be better documented through an observational note accompanied by photos and/or work samples?

Group Discussion: Share the standards identified for each category. Check that they fit the criteria identified above. Then, once you have identified some standards in the quick-and-easy category, you can develop your own Quick Check Recording Sheets (as in the New Mexico model). We have given you a blank Quick Check Recording Sheet as handout 13.

• • • • • ◉ • • • • •

Documenting with Portfolios

Portfolio documentation can be a way to show children's progress on standards. Portfolio forms were designed for teachers in the New Mexico PreK Programs to document a selection of the PreK Essential Indicators. On them teachers write an observation note and attach any appropriate photos and/or work samples. Each form is designed to document one early learning indicator and includes the three steps of progress or rubric ratings. The teacher circles the rating that reflects the child's performance at a particular point in time. An example is shown on page 93.

New Mexico
pre K
Invest A Little
Get A Lot

New Mexico PreK
Focused Portfolio Collection Form

Child's Name_____Date_____Observer_____

Domain: NUMERACY
Early Learning Indicator: EI #12 Uses numbers and counting as a means for solving problems and determining quantity.

Child's Progress towards the Outcome: *Circle the appropriate rating*

First Steps	**Making Progress Towards the Outcome**	**Accomplishing the Outcome**
Recognizes more or less (but does not count the objects) in a variety of situations.	Counts objects (not necessarily with one-to-one correspondence) in order to resolve a problem.	Counts objects with awareness of quantity and one-to-one correspondence in larger quantities in order to resolve a problem.

Check off whatever applies to the context of this observation:

❑ Child-initiated activity	❑ Done independently	❑ Time spent (1-5 mins.)
❑ Teacher-initiated activity	❑ Done with adult guidance	❑ Time spent (5-15 mins.)
❑ New task for this child	❑ Done with peer(s)	❑ More than 15 mins.
❑ Familiar task for this child		

Anecdotal Note: Describe what you saw the child do and/or heard the child say.

©Gronlund 2006 adapted from Gronlund and Engel 2001   *DRAFT July 2006*

You can help teachers determine children's levels of progress by analyzing portfolio documentation such as this and practice assigning the rubric rating that best fits the child's performance. Directions for this process are found in Staff Development Activity 21, "Rating Children's Performance by Reviewing Portfolio Documentation."

Staff Development Activity 21

Rating Children's Performance by Reviewing Portfolio Documentation

Purpose: To see examples of portfolio documentation and to practice rating children's progress on specific standards.

What to Do: See PowerPoint slides 46 and 47. See handout 14.

Using the portfolio samples in handout 14 or some from your own program, have participants read through the observation note and look at the additional context information (the checkbox in the middle of the form), as well as any accompanying photos or work samples. Then ask them to decide which of the three levels they would assign for this child's performance. Encourage them to consider for which level they have clear evidence of the child's capabilities. They cannot guess or assume—they must determine that the evidence firmly supports the rating.

Group Discussion: Encourage discussion that focuses on the evidence seen in the description of the child's actions and comments that supports the ratings given. Again, complete agreement is not necessary. Ask the following questions:

- What did you see the child do or hear the child say that led you to your rating?
- Was it difficult to figure out that rating? What factors did you have to take into consideration?

Assessing What Each Child Can Do, Rather Than Cannot Do

Observing children for what they can do helps teachers build a much more accurate case about the child's capabilities. We find that some teachers struggle with moving beyond a "checklist mentality" when assessing children's growth. They think of assessment as a series of tasks that every child must complete in the same way. They set up an activity and require every child to participate. The teacher then checks off whether the child is able to complete the activity or demonstrate the skill involved. This is not considered authentic assessment because these are on-demand tasks which are really in a form of a test, often given with only one possible time to demonstrate achievement. A child may perform at a higher or lower level on that particular day and at that particular moment, compared to what he typically does day in and day out. A child then may "fail" the assessment or show skills beyond what she has done before. In the video vignette suggested for use with Staff Development Activity 22, the child, Sydney, does not succeed in putting together a puzzle. If a teacher only assessed her performance in that incident with a checklist item related to problem solving with puzzles, she might give Sydney's puzzle skills a failing grade. However, Sydney does show other capabilities in this vignette (such as persistence and tolerance of frustration). We want to encourage teachers to not limit their observations in such a way that children's successes are overlooked. We want teachers to assess what children can do rather than what they cannot do. Staff Development Activity 22, "A Focused Observation on Problem Solving," uses the video vignette of Sydney to illustrate this point.

Staff Development Activity 22

A Focused Observation on Problem Solving

Purpose: To practice moving beyond a "checklist mentality" and observe what a child can do.

What to Do: See PowerPoint slides 48 and 49.

Using the DVD accompanying this book, play vignette 5, "Working with a Puzzle," which shows Sydney (4 years 10 months) and Jaiden (5 years 1 month). Ask the participants to watch, paying close attention to Sydney's problem-solving capabilities with the puzzle. Ask them to write down what they see, and remind them to be factual and descriptive, not interpretive, in their observation notes. After writing the documentation, have them look at their state's early learning standards and identify one related to problem solving skills.

Group Discussion: In the vignette, Sydney is not very successful with the puzzle. She continually places the pieces in the wrong places, turning them this way and that, but never placing them correctly. In your discussion with your group, point out that if you were limiting your assessment of Sydney's actions to her problem-solving skills only, you would probably assess her at a low level of proficiency. However, encourage the participants to look at other skills and capabilities that Sydney demonstrated. For example, she did not get frustrated; she allowed Jaiden to help her; she stayed focused on the task, showing persistence. This kind of discussion helps teachers recognize that often they can gain more information by observing beyond the checklist item (in this case, problem solving with puzzles) and see the approaches to learning that a child is successful in demonstrating. Use the following questions to guide the discussion:

- What did Sydney show that she could do?
- Were there similarities and differences in the documentation from the group? Did people see different capabilities? Why do you think that is?
- What would your next steps be to help Sydney with problem solving and puzzles?

• • • • • ◉ • • • • •

Building a Case about a Child across Several Domains

In reality, one observation alone does not create a full, rich picture of a child's strengths, learning styles, and interests. Even if a teacher is trying to do some quick and easy documentation, she still observes a child on multiple occasions, looking for how the child is growing in a variety of domains or areas of learning. She doesn't document all of her observations. If she did, she would go through reams and reams of paper! Instead she chooses the instances that are important to help her build a case about the child. "This is the all-important task of an early educator: reflecting on what you are learning about a child and figuring out what you are going to do for him" (Gronlund and James 2005, 121). Staff development activities can provide teachers with the opportunity to review multiple observations and build a case about a child's accomplishments and interests. You can use multiple video vignettes of the same child or a collection of observations about a child to do this type of reflection, as in Staff Development Activity 23, "Building a Case about a Child across Domains."

Staff Development Activity 23
· ·
Building a Case about a Child across Domains

Purpose: To have teachers practice pulling together information across domains about a child in order to assess his development and plan learning activities that will best meet his needs.

What to Do: See PowerPoint slides 50–52. See handout 15.

Using the DVD accompanying this book, play vignette 6, "Making Music," vignette 7, "Listening to a Story," and vignette 8, "Playdough, Cups, and Binoculars," all of which show Christian (2 years 7 months). Or you can use the collection of anecdotes about Claudia found in handout 15. If you use the video clips, have your teachers observe Christian doing the activities, and take notes about the things he does. As an alternative, ask them to read through the anecdotes about Claudia. Then ask them to answer the following questions:

- What can and does this child do? What are the child's interests and how does he/she show them? What specific skills does the child have?
- What would the next steps be for the child in her/his development? What is the child not doing yet?
- What would you plan to do to help the child build on his/her strengths and interests and to work on what he/she is not doing yet? What materials, activities, teacher support, peer support, and special resources would you use?

Ask them to reflect on their ideas about the child's accomplishments, interests, and needs, to identify the next steps that they would plan for the child, and to be prepared to share their thinking with others.

Group Discussion: Ask members of the group to share their ideas about the child's accomplishments, interests, and needs. Compare the next steps that were planned for Christian and/or Claudia.

• • • • • ◉ • • • • •

Using Observations to Improve Teaching

While assessment of children's progress is a critical reason for observing children, the primary purpose for observational assessment is to improve teaching. Teachers observe so they can individualize curriculum for each child. We find that this topic is best addressed in follow-up sessions with teachers who are implementing observational assessment. In such sessions, we ask teachers to identify their successes and challenges when observing children's progress. Inevitably we hear many comments about lack of time and problems with organizational management. We also hear concerns about integrating early learning standards into the assessment process. Often these concerns reflect the teachers' unfamiliarity with the wording of the standards and the specific skills or traits that they address. We also frequently hear comments about successes. We think these comments show the important steps that teachers are taking to improve their teaching. Teachers have told us:

> *"I know my children so much better than I did."*
> *"Observing is helping me focus in on individual children when before, I thought more about the group as a whole."*
> *"We are more aware of what the children can and can't do. We listen more carefully to what they try to communicate to us."*

In addition, when asked to reflect on integrating early learning standards into their curriculum more deliberately, teachers have responded:

> *"The early learning standards have focused our activities and centers."*
> *"We are more aware of what our lessons and activities are lacking."*
> *"Once we planned, we saw that the standards came out on their own in the children's interactions with materials and each other."*
> *"The early learning standards made us more aware of what our students' specific skills were within our lessons."*

These comments reflect how deeply assessment influences and affects curricular strategies. As we have said before, the two are integrated in ongoing and ever-changing ways. Again, you can refer to the graphic shown here to demonstrate the cyclical nature of the assessment and curriculum process.

We find that it is important to help teachers relate assessment to teaching. We incorporate Vygotsky's work (Berk and Winsler 1995) and ask teachers to reflect on observations and identify individual children's Zone of Proximal Development (ZPD). We remind them that the ZPD is evident when a child is beginning to try out a new skill

The Assessment and Curriculum Process

1 Observe and document what you see *(evaluate your plan)*

2 For an individual child: Ask *"What can I do to help this child?"*
For the whole group: Ask *"What is working? What is not?"*

3 Formulate a plan

4 Implement a plan

or demonstrate a new understanding but needs another person's help in order to be successful. The child is not competent enough yet to do the action independently. A teacher's role then is to determine how best to support the child in his ZPD so that he can move toward independence and competence. Vygotsky uses the term "scaffolding" to refer to the adult role here. If you think of a scaffold at a construction site, you picture a structure that protects workers from falling. In helping children to take risks in trying new things, teachers are providing protection from failing to children and offering them support as they try something new. The art of teaching involves determining when to pull back and remove the scaffold because the child is able to do the task on his own. In Staff Development Activity 24, "You've Observed the Children: So Now What?" teachers reflect on their observations and identify individual children's Zone of Proximal Development. They then determine how best to scaffold and support the child in his ZPD so that he can move toward independence and competence related to that skill or concept.

Staff Development Activity 24

You've Observed the Children: So Now What?

Purpose: To help teachers consider using information gained by observing children to better plan ways to support and scaffold new learning.

What to Do: See PowerPoint slides 53–56. See Handouts 16a and 16b.

Using handouts 16a and 16b, discuss the definition of the Zone of Proximal Development (ZPD) with your group. One way to define ZPD is the "place where children do not quite have independent skills, but where they can be successful with adult or peer support. . . . When a task is within a child's ZPD, the child can become more and more independent in completing it" (Gronlund and James 2005, 101–102). Berk and Winsler (1995, 26) define the adult's role in scaffolding or supporting a child in her ZPD:

> *According to Vygotsky, the role of education is to provide children with experiences that are in their ZPDs—activities that challenge children but can be accomplished with sensitive adult guidance. Consequently, adults carry much responsibility for making sure that children's learning is maximized by actively leading them along the developmental pathway. The teacher's role, rather than instructing children in what they are ready for or giving them tasks for which they have already acquired*

the necessary mental operations, is to keep tasks in children's ZPDs, or slightly above their level of independent functioning.

Group Discussion: Ask the group members to describe times when they have observed children and figured out their ZPD. Ask what they did to support them. Invite participants to give ideas to each other regarding ways to scaffold activities that will continue to challenge children in moving forward in their accomplishments.

• • • • • ⬤ • • • • •

In the next chapter we will give coaching and mentoring strategies to help you guide teachers as they take on changes in curriculum and assessment practices.

References

Berk, Laura E., and Adam Winsler. 1995. *Scaffolding children's learning: Vygotsky and early childhood education.* Washington, D.C.: National Association for the Education of Young Children.

Bowman, Barbara T. 2006. Standards at the heart of educational equity. *Young Children* 61(5):42–48.

Gronlund, Gaye. 2006. *Make early learning standards come alive: Connecting your practice and curriculum to state guidelines.* St. Paul: Redleaf Press.

Gronlund, Gaye, and Marlyn James. 2005. *Focused observations: How to observe children for curriculum and assessment.* St. Paul: Redleaf Press.

New Mexico PreK early learning outcomes. www.newmexicoprek.org. Accessed June 1, 2007, at www.newmexicoprek.org/index.cfm?event=public .prek.Materials.

Addressing Resistance to Changes in Curriculum and Assessment through Coaching and Mentoring

You may see that teachers exhibit resistance to changes in curriculum and assessment in many different ways. Being more intentional about children's learning—and at the same time recognizing the importance of allowing children to show, in the natural course of play, *how* they are learning—is a complex process. It requires constant watchfulness, a growing knowledge of each child's personality and capabilities, and quick, on-the-spot decision making to adapt activities and change teaching strategies and observational techniques as needed. Whew! Teaching young children can be exhausting! And for all of the same reasons, it can be very rewarding and interesting. That is what leaders in early education must keep at the forefront when attempting to bring about changes in curricular and assessment practices.

We recommend that you address resistance to change by coaching and mentoring teachers in their classrooms. This allows you to individualize your work to meet each teacher's needs and work with her personality and teaching style. It encourages her to show you how she is making attempts to integrate the concepts and ideas explored in staff development sessions. It also gives you the opportunity to see the challenges she is facing with specific children, classroom management, or the flow of her daily routine. In addition to observing, you can model and demonstrate alternate approaches as you spend time with the children and her. In this chapter, we identify ways that teachers may show resistance to change in both curriculum and assessment, and give you ideas for coaching strategies.

Resistance to Change in Curriculum

You may see resistance take several different forms as you observe and coach teachers in embracing new ideas about curriculum and the integration of early learning standards. We will identify four possible forms that resistance may take and give you some ideas for coaching strategies.

Form of Resistance #1: A teacher has been asked to show how early learning standards are being incorporated in her lesson or activity plans, and yet her plans include a list of materials or "cute" activities without including stated goals for the children's learning.

Coaching Strategies: One way to work with this resistance is to meet individually with the teacher and discuss what she wants the children to learn and gain from her planned activities. In our experiences with such discussions, we often find that the teacher is very clear in her mind about her expectations for the children's learning. For example, in one coaching session, a very experienced teacher, Julie, stated, "But I know it in my head. I just don't write it down." We see that our job, then, is to show her the value of writing down goals. As we talked with Julie, we pointed out that by writing goals or standards on her lesson plans, she could better communicate with parents. She recognized that this would help with questions parents asked about whether her program was "academic enough" for their children to be ready for kindergarten. She could communicate more clearly to them that even though the children were playing, there was purpose and thought involved in the experiences and the way that she was facilitating them. She also saw the benefit of being more explicit about goals for her building principal, who sometimes questioned the amount of play in her curriculum.

We recommend that when a teacher identifies goals in such a conversation, you write them down as they are discussed. You become the scribe. You are modeling the way goals should be written on a lesson plan and validating the teacher's thinking about children's learning. Occasionally, you may have a teacher whose stated goals are not related to standards. For example, she may have planned for marble painting in the art area "because it's fun." You can agree that activities should indeed be engaging and fun for children. Then you can point out that we can go beyond fun and identify what goals or early learning standards could be addressed. Generating a list of possibilities (fine motor control, vocabulary related to describing the marble's movements, the mixing of colors of paint, and so on) can help her to see more clearly how to address standards in beloved and fun activities.

Form of Resistance #2: Goals are written in a teacher's lesson plans but when you observe, you do not see any evidence of them implemented in the classroom.

Coaching Strategies: We find that by observing in the classroom, we are able to bring more to conversations with teachers that help them implement goals more clearly. After observing in the classroom, we suggest that you converse with the teacher involved and ask for the ways that she felt she was addressing goals in the activities you witnessed. You can bring up specific incidents with different children and talk about how the identified goal could have been addressed. You can make suggestions for materials that could have been added, or teacher comments that would have supported children's learning related to the identified goals. You can help her to see other possibilities that are more intentional. Together you can generate lists of open-ended questions and comments that she could have used.

Form of Resistance #3: The only time a teacher pays attention to goals and early learning standards is during teacher-directed activities such as large or small group times. The teacher expects the children to sit passively, listen quietly, and receive the information from her. Or, monotonous and repetitive skill work is substituted for playful exploration.

Coaching Strategies: Again, we find that observing and debriefing are valuable. In conversing with a teacher in this situation, you can refer back to the staff development sessions that focused on ways to incorporate early learning standards in children's play and investigation as well as in daily routines. It's very helpful to print out the charts of early learning standards that teachers generated for each of the learning areas (see Staff Development Activity 8 on page 64) as well as the daily routine webs (see Staff Development Activity 9 on page 66). Then you can refer to these in discussions with the teacher to help her expand her thinking. You can encourage her to see that every minute in an early childhood program has the potential to be a learning minute. And you can state your expectations about seeing evidence of her attention to learning at all times in future classroom observations.

Form of Resistance #4: A teacher writes early learning standards on activity plans and you may see that they are being addressed in the classroom, however, there is no indication that the teacher's implementation of them is fluid and changing as the children's capabilities change. Instead, the same goals are evident each week and children's behavior may show their boredom or lack of interest as they desire more challenging and interesting ways of learning.

Coaching Strategies: We have found that teachers are very anxious for help and support when children's behavior is difficult to manage and guide. You can use this to your advantage by helping teachers see that children's behavior is deeply influenced by the activities that are available to them. In conversing with a teacher in this situation, you can refer to the Teaching Continuum (in handout 1a on page 118) and to the discussions around levels of child engagement (Staff Development Activities 1, 2, 3 and 4 on pages 49–55). You can remind her that her planned activities should be changing and dynamic in such a way that they are meeting children at just the right level to engage their attention and capture their interest. The following story is an example of a coaching session that addressed this issue.

Mary Anne was a teacher of three- and four-year-olds. She wrote lesson plans that included early learning standards and goals for all activities and routines. Yet her supervisor, Ella, worried that she often did not follow through with adjusting those plans to meet the needs of the children, as behavior problems were frequent in her classroom. Ella became concerned when she saw the children's behavior when engaging in the following activity. For two to three weeks, Mary Anne filled the sensory table with sand each day. Along with the sand, she provided small plastic shovels and containers. She identified the goal of this activity as scientific and mathematical in nature: the children would explore the properties of sand and estimate how many scoops would be needed to fill various containers. From the very first day, children's engagement at the sensory table was not positive. Safety became an issue as children began to dig with more and more vigor; the sand was going everywhere, including in children's eyes and on the floor. Children were slipping on the spilled sand. Children's voices grew high-pitched, their digging grew more forceful, their giggles and howls more hysterical. Mary Anne and her colleague would try to stay nearby and encourage them to be more gentle in their actions and to describe what the sand looked and felt like, but to no avail. The same behavior happened each day. And yet the same activity was provided for two weeks.

After observing in the classroom, Ella discussed with Mary Anne why she thought the activity deteriorated so quickly. Together, they looked at the Teaching Continuum and discussed the levels of child engagement. They both agreed that the activity was child-directed and that the teaching strategies had been ones of acknowledging, modeling, and facilitating. They also agreed that the activity was not successfully engaging children to explore the properties of sand in a safe and productive way. Ella wondered if there was a way to scaffold the children's work with the sand in such a way to add higher intellectual involvement and clearer goals. She pointed out that such goals could give the children a more defined reason to dig in the sand and increase the safety of the activity. She suggested that Mary Anne bury small animals and dinosaurs in the sand. Ella also suggested that Mary Anne read books with the children about archaeology and how animal remains are found buried in soil, giving scientists information about life on earth at those times. Finally, she suggested that instead of shovels and containers, the children be given smaller tools that would require more fine-motor skills with which to dig (such as small paintbrushes and spoons). Then, once the items were found in the sand, further activities could take place such as sorting and categorizing what was found, and charting the whole experience in a class book or story chart. Now, multiple goals had been woven into the activity. In order to help the children work toward those goals, Mary Anne and her colleague had to change their teaching strategies on the Teaching Continuum as well. Now, they would be co-constructing with the children, continually helping them to add complexity to the activity and to increase its intellectual engagement and physical challenge, thus settling the behavior down. Mary Anne reported very positive results.

There may be other ways that you see resistance to change in evidence with teachers. Spending time in classrooms observing and modeling, then conversing with teachers, is an invaluable way to demonstrate your commitment to helping them embrace changes, take risks, and continue to grow and learn.

Addressing Resistance to Changes in Assessment

Working as a coach and mentor directly with a teacher in her classroom will help you individualize your work on assessment practices to meet each teacher's needs and work with her personality and teaching style. Working directly with a teacher encourages her to show you how she is making attempts to integrate the concepts and ideas explored in staff development sessions. It also gives you the opportunity to see the challenges she is facing with time management, a critical component of the observation and documentation process. We find that this is the most commonly named obstacle to implementing authentic assessment processes. Each teacher has to find her own way to organize her time and may have to try various methods until she feels comfortable. As a coach in her classroom, you can contribute your own observations to support her documentation efforts. You can also model ways of assessing children in a time-efficient manner. We think that, as we found in our experiences, you will see that teachers make changes in their curricular practices as they embrace authentic assessment procedures. Here again, assessment is driving curriculum, and in a positive and thoughtful way.

You may see resistance take several different forms as you observe and coach teachers in using authentic assessment as a means of integrating early learning standards into daily practice. We will identify two possible forms that resistance may take and give you many ideas for coaching strategies.

Form of Resistance #1: The most common complaint we hear about implementing observational assessment is that it takes too much time. We ask teachers to be more specific and identify the tasks they find time-consuming. The following list gives examples of the kinds of observation tasks that teachers identify as taking too much time:

- "It's hard to figure out when to fit in observation during a busy day with children."
- "It feels like it takes me away from the children."
- "I can't always write down an observation note right away. And memory lapses make waiting until later a problem."
- "It's hard to figure out the formats that work best for documenting what I see children do."
- "How much should I write in an observation note? How do I write just enough in a quick way to describe what a child does?"
- "Organizing my observation notes, photos, and work samples is a challenge."
- "It takes time to learn the standards or criteria that I will be using to evaluate the performance of the children that I have observed."

Coaching Strategies: Teachers often have difficulties figuring out when to fit in observation in the classroom because of a common misperception: Many teachers think that in order to observe children, the teacher must step out of the action and not interact with them in any way. We try to help teachers see that this does not have to be the case. In working with teachers in their classrooms, you can show them how observation is happening all the time: when a teacher and child are conversing, playing together, working on an activity together, and even when the teacher's back is turned! Teachers are listening, sensing, and watching children, continually taking in information from all parts of the classroom. They really do have eyes in the back of their heads. The problem is that in order to record what they are observing, they feel that they have to step away from their interaction with the child and concentrate on the documentation. And bringing early learning standards into the mix seems to only add to this misperception. As you observe and coach in their classrooms, we suggest that you help teachers learn ways to observe and document while they are involved with the children and model ways to include standards as well. You can do so by:

- being another set of eyes and ears
- introducing different types of documentation formats
- helping them organize their documentation
- asking them to include early learning standards on classroom signs, on displays of children's work, on bulletin boards, and in parent newsletters

Be Another Set of Eyes and Ears

First of all, helping teachers to see how much they do observe all day long is important. As a coach, you can visit the classroom and be another set of eyes and ears. You can write down some of the things that you and the teacher both observe. Then, as you debrief at the end of your visit, you can help the teacher evaluate the observations, determining what early learning standards are imbedded in the children's performance, and how best to keep track of the children's progress toward them. The observation notes you take may be added to the teacher's ongoing collection or to children's portfolios. You can also take photographs and collect work samples.

Different Formats for Different Teachers

Introducing teachers to different types of documentation helps them determine which methods work best with their own organizational style. And some documentation formats are best used right at the time of the observation, while others can be written at a later time. Teachers will have to try different things and will probably reject some of the methods. That's okay. They will be taking more ownership of the assessment process and developing comfort with their own documentation style. For example, some teachers might do better at writing lists of what children do because they tend to be list makers in other aspects of their lives. Some might prefer to take photos or to write very brief notes and then look at them after the children have left for the day. The photo or brief note jogs their memory so that they are able to write down what the child did and/or said at a later time. You can model ways to do a Quick Check Recording Sheet in activities with the children, as we showed on pages 90–91. Or you can be a teammate with the teacher and make notes as she reads a story or leads a large group. As you take notes in a classroom, you can model ways to write brief descriptions that still capture factually what the child did and/or said. If a teacher is writing long observation notes, you can help her edit them so that the essential information is included and the unnecessary details are eliminated. Encouraging teachers to find the methods that work best for them is an essential part of developing their competence as documenters of children's growth and learning.

Organizing Documentation

Some teachers feel overwhelmed by the organization of the documentation. They may write observations on sticky notes or index cards, but are unsure what to do with them. Some teachers take many photographs, and then are not clear about which ones should be used as documentation for assessment and which for displays. If portfolio formats (such as the New Mexico PreK Focused Portfolio Collection Form; see page 93) are being used, figuring out when to fill those out can be challenging for teachers. You can help them organize a filing system and determine when these tasks can be done. We recommend that a file folder be labeled for each child and placed in a milk-crate file container that is visible in the classroom. As a teacher writes an observation note, she can place it in the child's folder as soon as possible. We also recommend that if she writes the note in her neatest handwriting, she can then affix it with tape or glue it to a portfolio form and not have to rewrite it or type it. The 5-by-7-inch lined sticky notes that are available at office supply stores work very well for this purpose, as do index cards. If you are a director, you may want to consider giving teachers work time each week that is specifically dedicated to organizing documentation. Even half an hour a week is helpful. The HELP Program in Sunrise/Chapparal, New Mexico, calls this "Holy Time" and protects it from interruption. During this time teaching teams are to work together, discussing the things they have seen the children do that week, writing and editing observation notes, and preparing their portfolio documentation with accompanying photos and work samples.

Learning the Language of Standards

We have seen that another challenge of integrating early learning standards into the observational assessment process is learning the language of the standards. This takes time and practice. Many of the staff development activities we have suggested help teachers become more familiar with the criteria in your state's standards. However, seeing them come alive in children's actions is another story. Having teachers make signs with learning standards on them (as referred to on page 65) can help. Focusing discussions on ways that children are showing various standards allows teachers to consider different activities and times of day when standards can be addressed. These discussions can take place regularly in staff meetings as well as in individual coaching sessions.

Many teachers are creating documentation related to projects or studies that they are doing with the children as suggested by the Project Approach or the Reggio Emilia Approach. They are collecting children's drawings and writings, as well as taking photographs as children engage in long-term studies of topics of interest to them. As we noted in Staff Development Activity 12, these forms of documentation can be very rich in assessment information regarding early learning standards. In classroom visitations as well as staff meeting discussions, you can help them to look at their documentation of projects and studies to determine what progress the children are demonstrating toward early learning standards.

Bulletin Boards and Newsletters ~ Bulletin boards and parent newsletters can also be used to identify the standards that are being addressed in classroom activities. The process of creating them helps a teacher become more and more familiar with the standards herself. Julie Neff, a preschool teacher in Indiana, uses a bulletin board in the hallway of the elementary school where

she teaches to document the learning that is going on with her students. She posts photographs of the children engaged in exploration and play throughout the areas of her classroom and labels the photos with the learning goals that are being addressed. She ties those goals to the *Foundations to the Indiana Academic Standards for Young Children from Birth to Age 5*. Julie reports that this bulletin board has generated more comments than anything she has ever displayed. Not only do parents share their appreciation for the display, but also teachers and administrators in the building make positive comments. Even the preschool children themselves enjoy looking at the photo display. However, the group that has surprised Julie with their attention and feedback is the elementary-aged students who stand and study the photos, conversing among themselves about the things they see the preschool children doing. Julie routinely changes the photos and identifies different learning goals so that this display reflects the changing life of her classroom.

Julie's colleague, Melissa Merz, uses photos with identified learning goals in a different way: she creates a page of photos and attaches them to her weekly parent newsletter. Before doing so, Melissa had received some comments from family members asking why more paperwork done by the children was not coming home. Melissa tried to explain her philosophy that preschool children learn through hands-on manipulation of materials more than through paper and pencil tasks, but she wasn't sure the parents understood her explanation. Now that she sends home photos of the children in action on a weekly basis, the parent feedback has been very positive. Parents are no longer asking for paperwork, because they can see their children's learning in action!

Form of Resistance #2: Some teachers have a hard time imbedding observational assessment into children's play, exploration, and participation in daily routines. They still see curriculum and assessment as two completely separate parts of early childhood education. Therefore, when they do document what children are doing for assessment purposes, they tend to set up testing-tasks related to the skills or concepts they are assessing. Often the testing-tasks are teacher-directed rather than child-initiated and not related to the interests of the child. Children may have been pulled away from activities in which they were fully engaged in order to be assessed. Therefore, the validity of the assessment could be questioned. In addition, their documentation may look the same for each child, not reflecting each child's individuality and unique ways of demonstrating the skills.

Coaching Strategies: This type of resistance is usually not evident until teachers have done some documentation. We recommend that you include a periodic review of teachers' observational notes and portfolio samples as part of your role as a coach and mentor. When we do such reviews, we ask teachers to share with us a few of their notes and samples, encouraging them to choose two kinds:

1. Those they feel capture a child's actions and represent his or her typical development, in other words, the ones about which the teacher feels confident.

2. Those they struggled with in some way. Teachers may have found it hard to write down exactly what some children did and still be factual and descriptive. (This is often the

case when behavioral issues arise.) Or teachers may feel uncertain that they included all of the necessary information to assess a particular outcome or skill set.

Letting teachers choose which observations and samples to show you gives them some control over the sharing process. We find that asking for at least four to six in each of the categories gives us a good sense of how the documentation process is going for this teacher. Your coaching strategies will reflect what you learn from reviewing a teacher's documentation. You may:

- brainstorm ways to move beyond testing tasks and document standards in child-initiated activities or daily routines
- help teachers individualize descriptions of activities
- emphasize the importance of personal reflection

Moving Beyond Testing Tasks

When teachers show you notes or samples that appear to have been written and collected from a testing task rather than imbedded in more child-initiated activities and routines, you can brainstorm with them other ways in which a child might demonstrate the same skills or concepts. You can refer back to the lists generated for the classroom learning areas from Staff Development Activity 8 (see page 64) and the webs of early learning standards imbedded in daily routines from Staff Development Activity 9 (see page 66). You can also do some documentation yourself as you observe in the classroom. We find that teachers greatly appreciate our contributions in this regard. And it becomes a way for you to model various approaches to observational assessment.

Individualizing Documentation

If a teacher's documentation for several children looks formulaic, that is, the observation note for each child is written in almost exactly the same language as for the others, you can help her individualize her writing. Encourage her to include a description of the activity in which the children were engaged (which may be the same for several children's documentation), and add information to show the individuality and uniqueness of the child's participation in that activity. There is nothing wrong with beginning several children's observation notes by writing the same description of an activity as long as the child's actions and words are also included. Here's an example of a description that could be used as an introductory sentence for several children's documentation:

> *Today, the children mixed food coloring and water and then painted pictures with the colored water.*

A teacher could write this once and make photocopies for several children's documentation. Then, for each child, she would write more details about how he or she went about mixing and painting. Here are two examples:

> **Example 1:** Today, the children mixed food coloring and water and then painted pictures with the colored water. Jonah mixed yellow and blue. "Hey, it's green!" he said. Then he painted with the green paint. He painted with blue and red as well. "That made purple," he said.

> **Example 2:** Today, the children mixed food coloring and water and then painted pictures with the colored water. Kayla spent most of her time mixing the colors. She carefully used the eyedroppers to squeeze small amounts of the food coloring into the water and watched as the color trickled down into the water and changed color. She worked alone, not talking with anyone. When I sat down next to her, I asked, "What are you noticing, Kayla?" She whispered, "I'm making rainbows."

Encouraging teachers to review their documentation and make sure that it is individualized is an important coaching task. In that way teachers learn the power of their documentation to create a full and rich picture of each child's accomplishments, interests, learning dispositions, and personality.

The Importance of Reflection

As stated in chapter 3, we see reflection as an important part of the adult learning process. Encouraging teachers to reflect on their own changes in thinking regarding both curriculum and assessment and the integration of early learning standards can be part of the coaching and mentoring process. We suggest that you use the steps of progress referred to on pages 87–88 and ask teachers to assess their own progress in embracing new practices. Ask each one to think about specific steps that she has taken in regard to curriculum and assessment changes and rate herself on the following:

1. Is she taking first steps toward integrating early learning standards into her curricular and assessment practices or other new approaches to teaching?
2. Is she making progress toward integrating early learning standards into her curricular and assessment practices or other new approaches to teaching?
3. Is she successfully integrating early learning standards into her curricular and assessment practices or other new approaches to teaching?

We believe in lifelong learning and encourage an atmosphere of continual learning and improvement. So even if a teacher feels she is accomplishing the goals we have jointly set out, we encourage her to consider the next steps of accomplishment for herself. How will she continue to grow? What are some new areas that she will want to explore?

We recommend creating an atmosphere with expectations for change, where even the small steps that each person is taking are celebrated and supported. Discussing individual progress with teachers, as well as suggesting that they track their own progress through journaling and discussions with other teachers, will invite them to recognize and celebrate their own growth.

Coaching and mentoring in classrooms, in combination with effective and ongoing staff development sessions, can be a powerful combination. Both require careful planning as well as sensitivity and understanding of an individual teacher's strengths and personality traits. Just like the children, teachers will be at different places in their learning and growth and in their willingness to embrace changes and move forward in trying new things. Being a leader in this process asks us to do the same kind of integration of observation and assessment that teachers do with the children in their classrooms. We need to reflect on what we are seeing in the classrooms and ask ourselves questions about how best to help that teacher. We then move forward with plans and assistance, only to observe again.

Final Thoughts: Experiential Learning

In this book, we have focused on experiential learning. Kolb and Fry (1975) identify four elements of experiential learning:

1. concrete experience
2. observation and reflection
3. the formation of abstract concepts
4. testing in new situations

Even when we introduced new ideas in the staff development activities in this book, we tried to include ways for teachers to reflect on their own experiences with children in order to embrace and understand new concepts. And in the coaching strategies, we have suggested that you and a teacher work together in testing out new approaches and ways of teaching and assessing right in her classroom. We hope that you have gained some ideas for your work with teachers in staff development and coaching sessions. We encourage you to consider other ways that you can plan experiential learning for your teachers that includes the four elements listed above.

Change is a difficult process for many people. We can help others embrace the changes more readily by emphasizing that we are all on this journey together and that the practices we are learning and refining are right for young children. This takes commitment, passion, courage, and dedication on the part of staff development leaders, directors, and teachers. We firmly believe that the field of early childhood education benefits because of our collective willingness to explore new thinking, consider new research, and reevaluate teaching and assessment approaches, while at the same time remaining true to serving young children and their families in ways that are most helpful to them.

References

Indiana Department of Education and Family and Social Services Administration, Division of Family Resources, Bureau of Child Care. 2006. Foundations to the Indiana academic standards for young children from birth to age 5. Revised: August 2006. Accessed May 16, 2007, at www.doe .state.in.us/primetime/welcome.html#1.

Kolb, David A., and Roger Fry. 1975. Toward an applied theory of experiential learning. In *Theories of group process*, ed. C. Cooper. London: John Wiley.

Appendix A
Handouts for Staff Development Activities

The following pages show reduced-size versions of the handouts for the staff development activities in this book. These handouts are included here for your easy reference as you read through the chapters and activity descriptions. You will want to reproduce these handouts from the full-size versions found on the CD-ROM that accompanies this book. We hope this is helpful.

Teaching Continuum

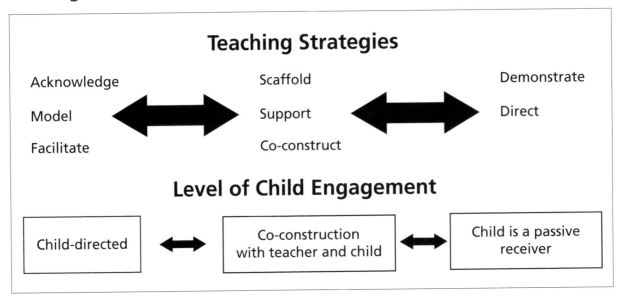

Throwing Colored Bears

Read the following and identify the possible teaching strategies that could be used to enhance the situation most fully for the children.

~~~~~~

Three four-year-old boys are invited by their teacher to sort colored bears into round sorting trays with multiple compartments. As long as the teacher is there with them, the boys cooperate in the sorting activity, talking about the colors of the bears as they sort them. As she moves on after five or six minutes to help in another area of the classroom, their interaction with the bears changes. "Hey, I know," says Alec. "Let's see who can throw them into the tray!" The boys move the trays to the opposite end of the table and begin to throw the bears. Their initial throws involve aiming at the small compartments. As bears fly across the table and land in the compartments, some of them bounce out again onto the table from the force of the throw. The boys laugh hysterically and continue to throw the bears harder and harder. Their laughter grows louder by the minute. Soon, bears are flying across the table and onto the floor. The boys' laughter is high-pitched. They pound on and lie across the table as each bear lands.

Possible interventions that a teacher could make, depending on her goal and the reactions of the boys involved, include:

~~~~~~

If the goal is Safety, the teacher may choose to Facilitate: You move toward the boys, reminding them to take good care of materials and not hurt each other. You stay nearby to make sure that they tone down their throwing.

If the goal is to Sustain the boys' interest and be safe, the teacher may choose to Model: You move toward the boys, reminding them to take good care of materials and not hurt each other. You sit down with them and offer suggestions to help them aim more carefully and throw more gently so that the bears land in the compartments. You might say things like: "What would happen if you threw your bears more gently? Will they stay in the compartment? Should we pull the tray a little closer and try that? Or would it help to move it to the floor and drop the bears from a standing position? How can we make this safer?"

If the goal is to Extend what they are doing, the teacher may choose to Scaffold and Support: You move toward the boys and ask, "How many bears will this particular compartment hold? Shall we count and see?" As the play calms down and more careful aim is taken, you introduce purpose to the actions that goes beyond just throwing. "I wonder how many bears you can drop or throw gently into this compartment." You stay with the boys to get this going and help them count. You watch closely to see if they take the play in this direction and do calm down.

If the goal is to Interrupt because the play does not calm down, the teacher may choose to Direct: You introduce some different ways to use the bears and sorting trays. "We need to stop throwing the bears because this is not safe. I'm afraid our sorting trays will get broken or someone in our room will get hit by a bear." You can then suggest other ways to use the bears and sorting trays. "Let's go back to sitting at the table and sorting the bears into the tray. Shall we sort by color or by size? I see little bears, medium bears, and big bears. I also see lots of different colors. Which way should we sort them?" You stay with the boys to get this going and help them sort. You watch closely to see if they take the play in this direction and do calm down.

If the goal is to Enrich and engage them for an even longer period of time, the teacher may choose to Co-construct: You can offer them a challenge. In the case of a sorting activity, one next step is to create patterns. You can model a simple pattern with two different colors of bears or two different sizes of bears in a repeating sequence. As you build your pattern, you say, "I'm going to challenge you! Can you figure out what I need to put next in my line of bears? Do you see how the color or size repeats? Can you make a line of bears like that?" You have now engaged them intellectually so that they are moving to higher levels of thinking and application of knowledge.

Balance Your Daily Schedule to Include Different Types of Activities

Breathing Out Times
(Early in day, after transitions,
at activity and choice times)
Open-ended, free-choice use of materials for
self-expression, movement, hands-on activity, creation,
construction, talking, singing, writing, drawing

Breathing In Times
(Small and large group activities,
focused investigations)
Listening, taking in new information, learning
new concepts, practicing skills with teacher
direction, focused choices and activities

Sample Daily Schedule for a Preschool Half-Day

8:00–8:25 AM Arrival Time

Children put away their backpacks and coats and go to tables where hands-on materials are available (greetings and conversation; writing and drawing; small manipulatives, such as Lego building blocks for constructing; and play-dough). *Breathing out*

8:25–8:45 AM Large Group Time

Children join in movement games, songs, and fingerplays *(breathing out)*, then listen to discussions and stories before planning for the day. *Breathing in*

8:45–10:00 AM Work or Activity Time

The children choose among a variety of learning areas and may be asked to join in a small group activity led by a teacher for approximately 10–15 minutes of this time. *More breathing out than anything; small group may be either breathing out or breathing in*

10:00–10:15 AM Cleanup Time

The children help clean up the entire classroom.

10:15–10:30 AM Snack Time

The children converse and eat snack. *Breathing out*

10:30–11:00 AM Outdoors

The children engage in a variety of large-muscle activities, outdoors if weather permits. *Breathing out*

11:00–11:15 AM Prepare to Go Home

Gather materials, backpacks, coats, and so forth. Review the day's activities and make plans for tomorrow.

11:15 AM Dismissal

Read through the following two scenarios and determine whether the teacher in each situation is sustaining children's engagement or interrupting it.

Scenario 1:

Three boys and one girl (all four-year-olds) are playing in the dramatic play area, putting scarves around their backs and calling them "magic capes." Ms. Denise helps them tie the scarves and asks them, "Why are the scarves magic?" Jacob responds, "Because they make us fly!" and proceeds to laugh loudly and run around the room. Eli and Luis follow him, bumping into each other, while Alejandra watches quietly. Ms. Denise says, "If you boys don't settle down, we'll have to take the scarves away. Why don't you come over here and play with Alejandra? I know! Your magic capes could be magic chef capes to help you cook a wonderful dinner." The boys continue to run around the room and Alejandra remains where she is.

Scenario 2:

Several three- and four-year-old children are seated at a table building with Duplos. Robbie and Bryce announce that they are making jet fighters and crash their constructions into one another, destroying them, and laughing. They then grab the pieces and build their "fighters" again. Teacher Racquel sits down and says, "Hey, tell me what's going on over here? What are you building?" Janie says, "I'm building a house." Racquel asks, "Where's the door? Oh, there it is. Who lives in your house, Janie?" As she and Janie talk, Robbie and Bryce crash their fighters again. Racquel says, "Boy, your fighters keep breaking apart when they crash. I wonder if there's a way to build them so that they are stronger. Did you know that the men and women who build airplanes have to work very hard to make their planes so that they are safe? How could you make your planes so that they are safe?" Racquel helps the boys choose parts and then test the connections and sturdiness without crashing. She explains that it's too expensive to do a crash test every time. The engineers have to do other kinds of tests. She then suggests that they take photographs of their different designs so they can remember them and display them for others to see. All of the children at the table start building their constructions and asking her to photograph them. They become much more interested in this aspect of the play and the crashing stops.

Early Learning Standard

"Children show interest and curiosity in counting and grouping objects and numbers."

—*Vermont Early Learning Standards: Guiding the Development and Learning of Children Entering Kindergarten*

Other states with a similar standard:
CA, CO, CT, DC, GA, IL, IA, LA, MD, MA, MI, MN, NE, NJ, NY, OK, RI, SC, TX, UT

Common Practices in an Early Childhood Classroom Where This Standard May Be Addressed

Counting throughout the day in daily activities and routines, in conversations indoors and out

Find as many ways as possible to make counting and numbers a part of every-day activities in the classroom! This can include counting the number of children present and absent, the number of boys and girls, the number of days in the week, the number of places at a table, the number of children in line, the number of blocks in a tower, the number of marks in a painting, the number of buttons on a jacket, the number of steps up the slide, the number of birds at the bird feeder, etc.

Access state standards at www.ccsso.org/ECEAstandards. For information correlating state standards, go to www.nieer.org/standards/statelist.php.

	First Steps Toward the Standard	Making Progress Toward the Standard	Accomplishing the Standard
What the Children Might Show You: *A range of interest, curiosity, and awareness of quantity*	Shows little interest or curiosity in counting or little awareness or accuracy when identifying quantities	Is beginning to count objects or people with awareness of quantity and one-to-one correspondence in small quantities	Is beginning to count objects or people with awareness of quantity and one-to-one correspondence in larger quantities
Curriculum and Activities that You Can Plan and Implement for Each Child's Progress Level	• As a child works and plays, converse back and forth about the quantities of objects, children, chairs, crackers, etc. • Include counting in daily routines of attendance, snack preparation, washing hands, and choosing learning areas. • Sing or chant fingerplays and songs with counting (such as "Three Green and Speckled Frogs"). • Accept the child's level of participation in these activities. Do not force the child to count so that a power struggle develops and the math experience becomes a negative one. • Make counting activities fun parts of every day.	• Continue to converse back and forth about the quantities of objects, children, chairs, crackers, etc., asking children to help you count. Start with small quantities. • Include counting in even more daily routines. • Sing or chant fingerplays and songs with counting (such as "Five Little Monkeys"). • Read counting books to large and small groups and individual children or count objects in books read. • Play counting games outdoors: Jump three times. Swing back and forth five times. • Encourage children to count throughout the day.	• Continue to increase the quantities of objects you converse about, sing about, read about, and incorporate in daily routines. • Play movement games that ask children to clap and count, stomp and count. "Simon says, 'Clap two times.'" Increase the quantities as children are able to follow through successfully. • Introduce numerals and help children see the connection between the symbol and the quantity. • Encourage children to count throughout the day to higher and higher quantities.

Early Learning Standard	Common Practices in an Early Childhood Classroom Where This Standard May Be Addressed

Access state standards at www.ccsso.org/ECEAstandards. For information correlating state standards, go to www.nieer.org/standards/statelist.php.

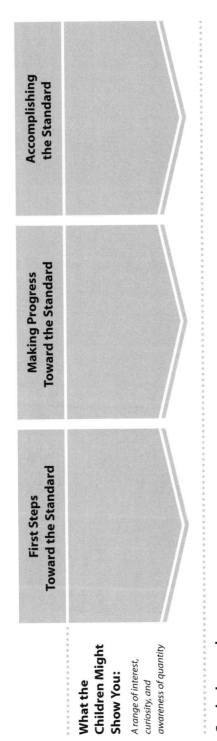

First Steps Toward the Standard

Making Progress Toward the Standard

Accomplishing the Standard

What the Children Might Show You:

A range of interest, curiosity, and awareness of quantity

Curriculum and Activities that You Can Plan and Implement for Each Child's Progress Level

Identifying Early Learning Standards for Classroom Learning Areas

Write the standards that children could be working on in specific areas in the classroom.

Art

Blocks

Identifying Early Learning Standards for Classroom Learning Areas

Sensory Table

Dramatic Play

Identifying Early Learning Standards for Classroom Learning Areas

Class Library

Manipulatives

Identifying Early Learning Standards for Classroom Learning Areas

Other

Writing Center

Standards and Daily Routines

Pick three daily routines and write one in the center of each blank web. Write in some of the early learning standards that can be addressed as children participate in each routine in the surrounding circles.

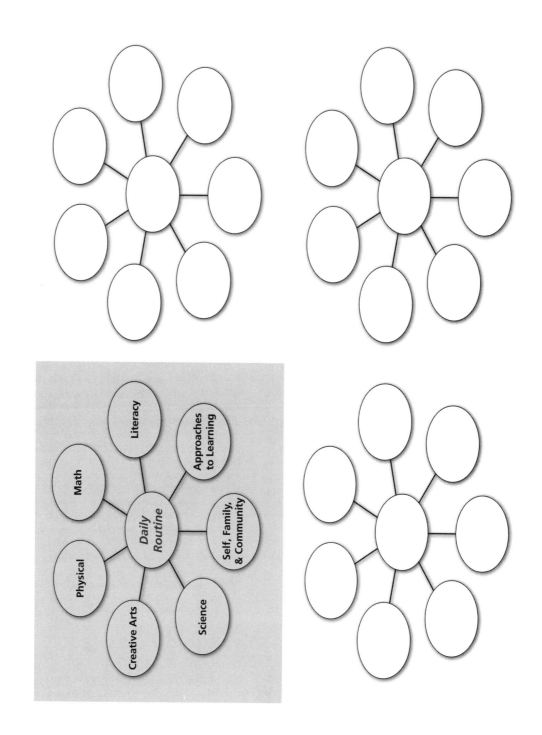

The Focused Early Learning Weekly Planning Framework

Date: _____   Teacher: _____

Child-led Exploration in the Rich Classroom Environment

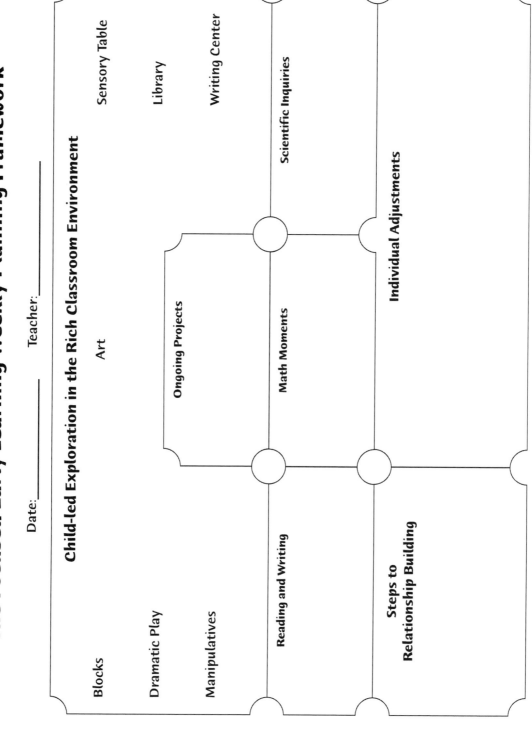

Blocks

Dramatic Play

Manipulatives

Art

Sensory Table

Library

Writing Center

Ongoing Projects

Reading and Writing

Math Moments

Scientific Inquiries

Steps to
Relationship Building

Individual Adjustments

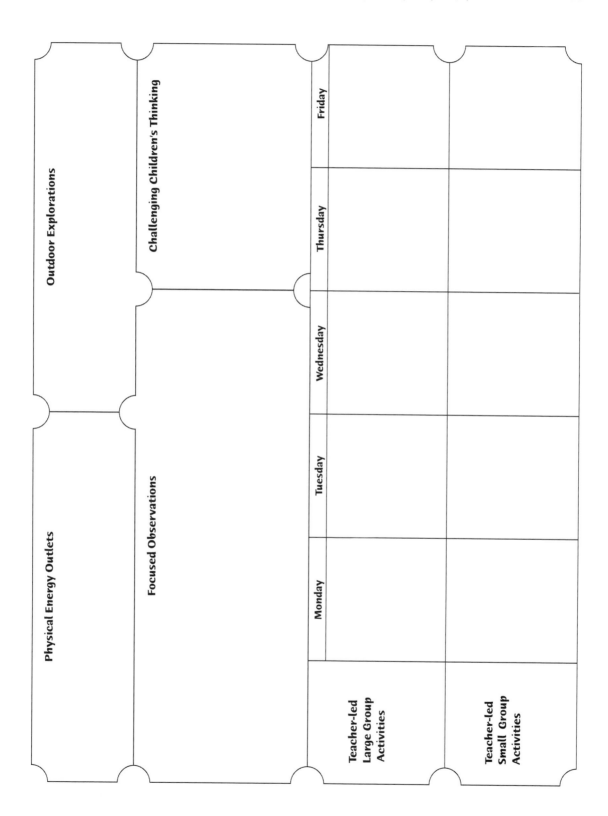

	Monday	Tuesday	Wednesday	Thursday	Friday
Teacher-led Large Group Activities					
Teacher-led Small Group Activities					

Physical Energy Outlets

Outdoor Explorations

Focused Observations

Challenging Children's Thinking

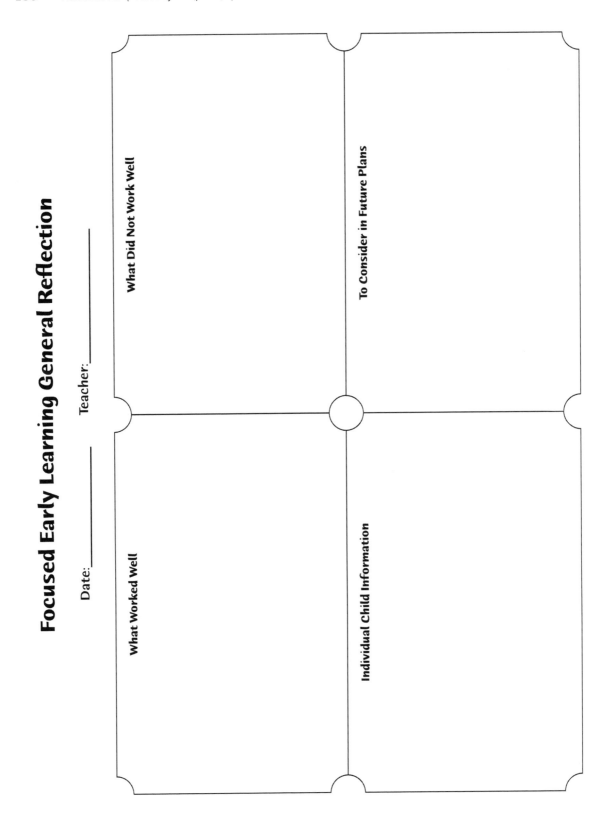

Focused Early Learning General Reflection

Date: _____   Teacher: _____

What Worked Well

What Did Not Work Well

Individual Child Information

To Consider in Future Plans

Lesson
Plan _____Delores_____   Date October 3-7, 2005

Letter of the Week: "D"

Seatwork: trace letter "D"
on sheet; decorate "D"
    with dots

Small group time!
make list of
"D" words
count how many
find something
that starts with
"D" in the room

Math:
Sort dinosaurs
by type — count.
Draw a picture of
    your favorite

Art
Color "D" coloring
pages

Fine Motor:
Cut out letter D's
& paste on sheet
Make "D"   out of
    playdough

Free Play:
play with
toys

Outdoors:
pretend to be "doggies" &
"dinosaurs"

Lesson
Plan _____ Rosie _____   Date September 2005

Free Play:
Paints at easel
Playdough

Songs:
"Twinkle, Twinkle"

"If You're Happy
& You Know It"

"Where is...?"
use names of
children

Free Play:
Wash baby dolls
at water table

SMALL GROUP:
Recognize
name cards,
name on cubby,
place at table, etc.

Books: The Kissing Hand
Going on a Bear Hunt

Free Play:
Legos/Duplos
Cardboard blocks

Outdoors:
Wagons, bikes, sand toys

The Focused Early Learning Weekly Planning Framework

Date: October 17-21 2005 Teacher: Suzette

Child-led Exploration in the Rich Classroom Environment

Blocks Cars & trucks

Dramatic Play Kitchen & dolls

Manipulatives leaf matching game

Art leaf rubbings

Sensory Table leaves & acorns

Library listening center

Writing Center markers & paper

Ongoing Projects

Fall Leaves

Reading and Writing read fall books

Math Moments count acorns

Scientific Inquiries Compare & contrast shapes & colors of leaves

Steps to Relationship Building Play "The Name Game"

Individual Adjustments

Keep Eric and Roberto separated at snack & circle.

Be ready to help Tianna separate from Grandma

Physical Energy Outlets

Greg & Steve - "Freeze" Game

Outdoor Explorations

rake leaves
if windy, scarves & streamers

Focused Observations

Record counting with acorns

Challenging Children's Thinking

Question of the Week:
Are leaves changing
color and/or falling
off at your house?

	Monday	Tuesday	Wednesday	Thursday	Friday
Teacher-led Large Group Activities	Song: "All the leaves are falling down" calendar			→	
Teacher-led Small Group Activities	Count acorns			→	

From *Early Learning Standards and Staff Development*. © 2008 Gaye Gronlund and Marlyn James. May be reproduced for classroom use only.

The Focused Early Learning Weekly Planning Framework

Date: Nov 14-18, 2005   Teacher: Maria

Child-led Exploration in the Rich Classroom Environment

Sensory Table
Flax seed for children to measure, pour, compare quantities.

Library
Read together {
"The Pumpkin Seed"
"Rain Makes Applesauce"
"All For Fall"
}

Writing Center
Children dictate stories & experiences with pumpkins, apples & family feasts. Illustrate.

Scientific Inquiries
Place rotting pumpkins in a clear container for children to observe. Keep an on-going journal of its changes.

Art
Encourage children's creating with collage materials: yarn, buttons, glitter, fabric & paper scraps.

Dramatic Play
Costume box for children to create their own costumes: fabric, scarves, hats, jewelry, shoes, capes, wands & pouches.

Manipulatives
To practice self help skills - provide boots & lacing boards; zippers & jackets to put on; mittens & gloves.

Blocks
Construct roads & ramps & measure how far balls, marbles & cars will go on them.

Ongoing Projects
Harvest

Math Moments
Sorting & classifying apples, squash, seeds, nuts, leaves, pinecones, herbs & flowers.

Reading and Writing
Read "Rain Makes Applesauce" - children follow pattern in the book. Make a picture recipe & follow to make applesauce.

Individual Adjustments
Help Aaron make positive choices at center time - then follow up & encourage him.
See if Mia will try the flax seed in the sensory table since it's not wet.

Steps to Relationship Building
Help children use "I feel" statements when conflicts arise.
Offer hugs or high fives.

Physical Energy Outlets

Set up the bean bag pumpkin game – children can try throwing over & under handed.

Outdoor Explorations

Collect leaves & twigs to add to collage materials. Give children 2, 3 & 4 step directions as an obstacle course.

Focused Observations

Note who catches on to pattern in "Applesauce" book.

Maria: Observe Aaron, Matthew, Josiah, Auggie & Joi

Lydia: Observe Antonio, Hanna, Thomas, Chase & Graciela

Challenging Children's Thinking

Challenge children to describe the similarities & differences between the sorting items (apple, squash etc.). Record their comments on a chart.

	Monday	Tuesday	Wednesday	Thursday	Friday
Teacher-led Large Group Activities	Sing gathering songs & play active games, then settle down. Read "Rain Makes Applesauce"	Look at rotting pumpkin. Discuss. Read "Pumpkin Seed"	Discuss sorting items & read through chart of comments	Reread "Rain Makes Applesauce". Have children help you	Tell something each child did this week. Reread "Pumpkin Seed"
Teacher-led Small Group Activities	Make applesauce. Help children "read" the picture recipe		Sort & classify items using a floorgraph or yarn circles.		Help children with self help skills with their own coats, boots, mittens, & gloves

Writing Anecdotes

Words and Phrases to Avoid	Words and Phrases to Use
• The child loves	• He often chooses . . . .
• The child likes	• I saw him . . . .
• He enjoys	• I heard her say . . . .
• She spends a long time at	• He spends five minutes doing . . . .
• It seems like	• She said . . . .
• It appears	• Almost every day he . . . .
• I thought	• Once or twice a month, she . . . .
• I felt	• Each time, he . . . .
• I wonder	• She consistently . . . .
• He does . . . very well	• We observed a pattern of . . . .
• She is bad at	
• This is difficult for	

What else can you add to these lists?

Using the chart in handout 9a, analyze the following anecdotes, identifying words and phrases that are interpretive or judgmental in nature and should be avoided. Try to edit each note and replace the interpretive words and phrases with ones that are factual, descriptive, and objective.

Jennifer (6 months)

Jennifer is a very fussy baby. She cries when her mom leaves. She demands a lot of adult attention. She has trouble settling down unless she has her pacifier or is being held. She startles easily and gets upset when other toddlers come near her.

Carrie (3 years 2 months)

Carrie runs outside to the bikes at riding time because she wants to have first choice of the bikes. She always wants the red bike and forgets the rule of walking outside to the bike area.

Max (2 years 6 months)

During art time today, Max really enjoyed painting a picture. He used up a lot of paint—green, blue, brown, and red. His picture is very interesting. It looks like he painted some people and a house. Max paints almost every day, and it seems to be his favorite activity.

Read the following description of Elijah in the block area and identify as many different conclusions about Elijah's actions as you can.

Elijah (3 years 9 months)

Elijah is in the block area. He has several animals in his hand. Several other children are in this area with him. He runs around in circles with the animals, and another child chases him. He laughs and screams, "You can't catch me!"

Read the following anecdote about JoAnngela (3 years 8 months). Identify the evidence that you see to support conclusions about her capabilities in the areas of cognitive, social, emotional, and physical development.

JoAnngela, Damien, and Adrianne sit down with me to read "The Three Little Pigs." JoAnngela sits for a while listening to the story. About halfway through the story, she gets on her knees and begins to rock back and forth. She bumps into Damien and tells him, "Sorry, Damien." She then stands up, moves to the other side of Adrianne, curls up on the beanbag, and finishes listening to the story.

Early Learning Standard

"Uses pretend writing during play activities (e.g., scribbles lines and shapes)"

—*California Desired Results for 3 Years through Prekindergarten*

Other states with a similar standard:
CO, CT, DC, GA, IL, IA, LA, MD, MA, MI, MN, MO, NY, OK, RI, TX, UT

Common Practices in an Early Childhood Classroom Where This Standard May Be Addressed

Providing many opportunities for children to play with writing tools and materials throughout the day

Young children love to imitate the adults in their lives. And adults write for many purposes in everyday life. Pretend writing is a way for children to experiment with the writing process before they feel confident in making recognizable letters and words. Even as they scribble, they are developing fine motor skills and their own awareness of the many purposes and reasons for writing in daily life.

Access state standards at www.ccsso.org/ECEAstandards. For information correlating state standards, go to www.nieer.org/standards/statelist.php.

	First Steps Toward the Standard	Making Progress Toward the Standard	Accomplishing the Standard
What the Children Might Show You: Many different ways of imitating adult writing, with increasing fine motor control and closer approximations to letter-like shapes or cursive writing	Makes random marks or scribbles for a variety of purposes	Identifies marks or scribbles as writing; shows more control of the writing tool	Purposefully makes marks and scribbles for writing purposes, with increasing control of the writing tool evident in the formation of letter-like shapes, perhaps even some letters, and forms of pretend cursive writing
Curriculum and Activities That You Can Plan and Implement for Each Child's Progress Level	• Model for the children how many ways you use writing every day. • Provide a variety of writing tools (markers, crayons, chalk, pens, pencils) and papers for children to experiment with writing. • Be sure to accept their scribbles and shapes as the writing that's just right for their age.	• Add writing tools and materials in the dramatic play area to give children opportunities to imitate writing grocery lists, recipes, letters, and phone messages as well as paying bills. • Be sure to accept their scribbles and shapes as the writing that's just right for their age.	• Set up a Writing Center in the classroom with many types of writing tools and papers. Add name cards, word lists, picture dictionaries, and alphabet posters for copying. • As children begin to be capable of writing recognizable letters, encourage them to do so. But also accept their scribbles and shapes.

Quick Check Recording Sheet with Steps of Progress

	Date & Activity	Date & Activity	Date & Activity	Date & Activity
Children's Names				
First steps (#1)				
Making progress (#2)				
Accomplished (#3)				

New Mexico PreK
Focused Portfolio Collection Form

Child's Name___Nathan_____**Date**__Sept. 4, '06_**Observer**__Joe_____

Domain: LITERACY
Essential Indicator: EI #7 Uses an increasingly complex and varied spoken vocabulary and sentence structure in language(s) used for instruction in the program.

Child's Progress towards the Outcome: *Circle the appropriate rating*

First Steps	**Making Progress Towards the Outcome**	**Accomplishing the Outcome**
Primarily uses single words in short combinations (phrases or one- to three-word sentences or the commands) occasionally using new vocabulary words in the child's home language.	Primarily uses phrases and sentences of three or four words, incorporating some new vocabulary words in the child's home language.	Primarily uses phrases and sentences of more than four words, incorporating many new vocabulary words in the child's home language with ever-increasing description and detail.

Check off whatever applies to the context of this observation:

☑ Child-initiated activity   ☐ Done independently   ☒ Time spent (1-5 mins.)
☐ Teacher-initiated activity ☒ Done with adult guidance ☐ Time spent (5-15 mins.)
☐ New task for this child   ☐ Done with peer(s)   ☐ More than 15 mins.
☑ Familiar task for this child

Anecdotal Note: Describe what you saw the child do and/or heard the child say.

"Me go, too." Nathan cried as his Mom dropped him off today. "No, mama. Stay," he called out as she walked down the hall. He sat in his cubby for a while. Whenever I checked on him, asking him if he would like to join me at a table activity, he shook his head and said, "No." After about five minutes, he came and sat on my lap at the playdough table. I hugged him and said, "You miss your Mom, don't you?" "Yes. Mama go to work." I assured him that she would pick him up after lunch time. He joined in with the others at the playdough table and continued with his day.

©Gronlund 2006 adapted from Gronlund and Engel 2001

DRAFT July 2006

New Mexico PreK
Focused Portfolio Collection Form

Child's Name____Jessica_____Date__Feb. 8, 2007__Observer **Maria**_____

Domain: LITERACY
Essential Indicator: EI #7 Uses an increasingly complex and varied spoken vocabulary and sentence structure in language(s) used for instruction in the program.

Child's Progress towards the Outcome: *Circle the appropriate rating*

First Steps	Making Progress Towards the Outcome	Accomplishing the Outcome
Primarily uses single words in short combinations (phrases or one- to three-word sentences or the commands) occasionally using new vocabulary words in the child's home language.	Primarily uses phrases and sentences of three or four words, incorporating some new vocabulary words in the child's home language.	Primarily uses phrases and sentences of more than four words, incorporating many new vocabulary words in the child's home language with ever-increasing description and detail.

Check off whatever applies to the context of this observation:

- ☐ Child-initiated activity
- ☒ Teacher-initiated activity
- ☐ New task for this child
- ☒ Familiar task for this child

- ☐ Done independently
- ☒ Done with adult guidance
- ☐ Done with peer(s)

- ☒ Time spent (1-5 mins.)
- ☐ Time spent (5-15 mins.)
- ☐ More than 15 mins.

Anecdotal Note: Describe what you saw the child do and/or heard the child say.

When it was Jessica's turn to share at circle time today, she told about her trip to the aquarium in Albuquerque over the weekend. "We saw sharks and they were swimming all around. And we saw turtles and lots and lots of colored fish. My Dad showed me some eels. They looked like snakes."

©Gronlund 2006 adapted from Gronlund and Engel 2001

DRAFT July 2006

New Mexico PreK
Focused Portfolio Collection Form

Child's
Name____Sam_____Date__3/14/07___Observer____Tara_____

Domain: LITERACY

Essential Indicator: EI #7 Uses an increasingly complex and varied spoken vocabulary and sentence structure in language(s) used for instruction in the program.

Child's Progress towards the Outcome: *Circle the appropriate rating*

First Steps	**Making Progress Towards the Outcome**	**Accomplishing the Outcome**
Primarily uses single words in short combinations (phrases or one- to three-word sentences or the commands) occasionally using new vocabulary words in the child's home language.	Primarily uses phrases and sentences of three or four words, incorporating some new vocabulary words in the child's home language.	Primarily uses phrases and sentences of more than four words, incorporating many new vocabulary words in the child's home language with ever-increasing description and detail.

Check off whatever applies to the context of this observation:

- ☑ Child-initiated activity
- ☐ Teacher-initiated activity
- ☐ New task for this child
- ☐ Familiar task for this child

- ☑ Done independently
- ☐ Done with adult guidance
- ☐ Done with peer(s)

- ☑ Time spent (1-5 mins.)
- ☐ Time spent (5-15 mins.)
- ☐ More than 15 mins.

Anecdotal Note: Describe what you saw the child do and/or heard the child say.

"Quiero mas papas, por favor. Me gusta mucho!" Sam is learning to speak Spanish in our class and is using more phrases with teachers and children. His home language is English and he converses frequently about things going on around him. Today, he explained the rules of a computer game to Grandma Jo, a classroom visitor. "See. First you have to click here on the arrow. Then, you drag it across so that you fill the basket all the way to the top."

New Mexico PreK
Focused Portfolio Collection Form

Child's
Name *Alegra*   Date *10/07/06*   Observer *Felicia*

Domain: LITERACY

**Essential Indicator: EI #7 Uses an increasingly complex and varied spoken vocabulary and
sentence structure in language(s) used for instruction in the
program.**

Child's Progress towards the Outcome: *Circle the appropriate rating*

First Steps	Making Progress Towards the Outcome	Accomplishing the Outcome
Primarily uses single words in short combinations (phrases or one- to three-word sentences or the commands) occasionally using new vocabulary words in the child's home language.	Primarily uses phrases and sentences of three or four words, incorporating some new vocabulary words in the child's home language.	Primarily uses phrases and sentences of more than four words, incorporating many new vocabulary words in the child's home language with ever-increasing description and detail.

Check off whatever applies to the context of this observation:

❑ Child-initiated activity   ❑ Done independently   ❑ Time spent (1-5 mins.)
☑ Teacher-initiated activity   ❑ Done with adult guidance   ☑ Time spent (5-15 mins.)
❑ New task for this child   ☑ Done with peer(s)   ❑ More than 15 mins.
❑ Familiar task for this child

Anecdotal Note: Describe what you saw the child do and/or heard the child say.

*Today Alegra listened with the other children to a story about Abiyoyo. She repeated the song
that was sung using Abiyoyo's name many times throughout the story. Later, as she played
in the dramatic play area, I heard her tell her friend, Sophia, "I liked that story. Abiyoyo
was funny." She then began to sing the song again and Sophia joined in. Both girls
smiled and giggled as they sang.*

©Gronlund 2006 adapted from Gronlund and Engel 2001   *DRAFT July 2006*

New Mexico PreK
Focused Portfolio Collection Form

Child's Name_____*Jonathan*__ Date___*9/27/06*__ Observer_____*Louise*_____

Domain: NUMERACY
Early Learning Indicator: EI #12 Uses numbers and counting as a means for solving problems and determining quantity.

Child's Progress towards the Outcome: *Circle the appropriate rating*

First Steps	Making Progress Towards the Outcome	Accomplishing the Outcome
Recognizes more or less (but does not count the objects) in a variety of situations.	Counts objects (not necessarily with one-to-one correspondence) in order to resolve a problem.	Counts objects with awareness of quantity and one-to-one correspondence in larger quantities in order to resolve a problem.

Check off whatever applies to the context of this observation:

❑ Child-initiated activity	☒ Done independently	❑ Time spent (1-5 mins.)
☒ Teacher-initiated activity	❑ Done with adult guidance	☒ Time spent (5-15 mins.)
❑ New task for this child	❑ Done with peer(s)	❑ More than 15 mins.
☒ Familiar task for this child		

Anecdotal Note: Describe what you saw the child do and/or heard the child say.

Jonathan helped pass out the snack today. He counted out two graham crackers for each child. When he sat down at his place, he spread peanut butter on his crackers and poured out his cup of raisins. As he placed each one on his cracker, he counted accurately up to seven. Then, his numbers got a little mixed up: "7, 9, 10, 12, 14." "I have 14," he said.

©Gronlund 2006 adapted from Gronlund and Engel 2001

DRAFT July 2006

New Mexico PreK
Focused Portfolio Collection Form

Child's Name _____ **Luis** _____ Date _**11/2/06**_ Observer _____ **Helena** _____

Domain: NUMERACY

Early Learning Indicator: EI #12 Uses numbers and counting as a means for solving problems and determining quantity.

Child's Progress towards the Outcome: *Circle the appropriate rating*

First Steps	**Making Progress Towards the Outcome**	**Accomplishing the Outcome**
Recognizes more or less (but does not count the objects) in a variety of situations.	Counts objects (not necessarily with one-to-one correspondence) in order to resolve a problem.	Counts objects with awareness of quantity and one-to-one correspondence in larger quantities in order to resolve a problem.

Check off whatever applies to the context of this observation:

- ☒ Child-initiated activity
- ☒ Teacher-initiated activity
- ☐ New task for this child
- ☒ Familiar task for this child

- ☒ Done independently
- ☒ Done with adult guidance
- ☐ Done with peer(s)

- ☐ Time spent (1-5 mins.)
- ☒ Time spent (5-15 mins.)
- ☐ More than 15 mins.

Anecdotal Note: Describe what you saw the child do and/or heard the child say.

Luis was stringing beads at the table today. He had placed several red beads in a pile in front of him. I asked him, "How many red beads do you have, Luis?" He looked at me and said, "I don't know." "Shall we count them together?" I asked. He shook his head "no." "I wonder if you have more red ones or more blue ones," I said. "I have lots more red!" he replied. And, he was right! This is typical for Luis at this time. He is not showing interest in counting yet.

New Mexico PreK
Focused Portfolio Collection Form

Child's Name_____Anna__Date____3/30/07__Observer____Nancy_____

Domain: NUMERACY
Early Learning Indicator: EI #12 Uses numbers and counting as a means for solving problems and determining quantity.

Child's Progress towards the Outcome: *Circle the appropriate rating*

First Steps	Making Progress Towards the Outcome	Accomplishing the Outcome
Recognizes more or less (but does not count the objects) in a variety of situations.	Counts objects (not necessarily with one-to-one correspondence) in order to resolve a problem.	Counts objects with awareness of quantity and one-to-one correspondence in larger quantities in order to resolve a problem.

Check off whatever applies to the context of this observation:

- ☐ Child-initiated activity
- ☒ Teacher-initiated activity
- ☐ New task for this child
- ☒ Familiar task for this child

- ☐ Done independently
- ☒ Done with adult guidance
- ☐ Done with peer(s)

- ☒ Time spent (1-5 mins.)
- ☐ Time spent (5-15 mins.)
- ☐ More than 15 mins.

Anecdotal Note: Describe what you saw the child do and/or heard the child say.

It was Anna's turn to count how many children were present today. She started to walk around the circle, counting out loud, "1, 2, 3, 5, 7, 9." She sometimes skipped a child as she went. I stood up and helped her start from the beginning. Together, we patted each child's back as we counted them.

©Gronlund 2006 adapted from Gronlund and Engel 2001

DRAFT July 2006

New Mexico PreK
Focused Portfolio Collection Form

Child's Name_____ Amy ___Date____ 2/16/07 _Observer ___ Brie _____

Domain: NUMERACY
Early Learning Indicator: EI #12 Uses numbers and counting as a means for solving problems and determining quantity.

Child's Progress towards the Outcome: *Circle the appropriate rating*

First Steps	Making Progress Towards the Outcome	Accomplishing the Outcome
Recognizes more or less (but does not count the objects) in a variety of situations.	Counts objects (not necessarily with one-to-one correspondence) in order to resolve a problem.	Counts objects with awareness of quantity and one-to-one correspondence in larger quantities in order to resolve a problem.

Check off whatever applies to the context of this observation:

☑ Child-initiated activity   ☑ Done independently   ☑ Time spent (1-5 mins.)
☐ Teacher-initiated activity ☐ Done with adult guidance ☐ Time spent (5-15 mins.)
☐ New task for this child   ☐ Done with peer(s)   ☐ More than 15 mins.
☑ Familiar task for this child

Anecdotal Note: Describe what you saw the child do and/or heard the child say.

Amy was lining up at the door to go outside when she announced, "Teacher Brie, we have two more girls than boys in our class!" "How do you know, Amy?" "Because I counted them. See: 1,2,3,4,5,6,7,8 girls and 1,2,3,4,5,6 boys." She said this as she tapped each child on the shoulder.

©Gronlund 2006 adapted from Gronlund and Engel 2001

DRAFT July 2006

New Mexico PreK
Focused Portfolio Collection Form

Child's Name _____*Chase*_____ Date__*2/2/07*___ Observer___*Maria*___

Domain: SCIENTIFIC CONCEPTUAL UNDERSTANDINGS
Early Learning Indicator: EI #17 Uses senses to investigate characteristics and behaviors in the physical and natural worlds and begins to form explanations of observations and explorations.

Child's Progress towards the Outcome: *Circle the appropriate rating*

First Steps	Making Progress Towards the Outcome	Accomplishing the Outcome
Uses obvious sensory information to explore the world, reacting more physically than verbally.	Uses senses to explore the world (not just through the obvious), making 1 – 2 simple comments describing sensory experiences.	Uses multiple senses to explore the world and makes 1 or more detailed comments describing sensory experiences.

Check off whatever applies to the context of this observation:

- ☑ Child-initiated activity
- ☐ Teacher-initiated activity
- ☑ New task for this child
- ☐ Familiar task for this child

- ☑ Done independently
- ☐ Done with adult guidance
- ☐ Done with peer(s)

- ☐ Time spent (1-5 mins.)
- ☐ Time spent (5-15 mins.)
- ☑ More than 15 mins.

Anecdotal Note: Describe what you saw the child do and/or heard the child say.

Chase spent most of the activity time today exploring the "clean mud" that we had made with tissues, water and soap in the sensory table. He made many comments about how it felt, looked and smelled:

"This is slimy. See? It bunches together when you squeeze it but when you lift it up, it falls down. Mmmm...this smells good. Like soap."

DRAFT July 2006

New Mexico PreK
Focused Portfolio Collection Form

Child's Name _____ Bailey _____ Date __3/10/07__ Observer ___ Robin ___

Domain: SCIENTIFIC CONCEPTUAL UNDERSTANDINGS
Early Learning Indicator: EI #17 Uses senses to investigate characteristics and behaviors in the physical and natural worlds and begins to form explanations of observations and explorations.

Child's Progress towards the Outcome: *Circle the appropriate rating*

First Steps	**Making Progress Towards the Outcome**	**Accomplishing the Outcome**
Uses obvious sensory information to explore the world, reacting more physically than verbally.	Uses senses to explore the world (not just through the obvious), making 1 – 2 simple comments describing sensory experiences.	Uses multiple senses to explore the world and makes 1 or more detailed comments describing sensory experiences.

Check off whatever applies to the context of this observation:

- ❏ Child-initiated activity
- ☒ Teacher-initiated activity
- ☒ New task for this child
- ❏ Familiar task for this child

- ❏ Done independently
- ☒ Done with adult guidance
- ❏ Done with peer(s)

- ❏ Time spent (1-5 mins.)
- ☒ Time spent (5-15 mins.)
- ❏ More than 15 mins.

Anecdotal Note: Describe what you saw the child do and/or heard the child say.

During our cooking activity, today, Bailey took a little taste of salt, of sugar, of flour and ate a chocolate chip. "I like the chocolate the best!" she said.

**New Mexico PreK
Focused Portfolio Collection Form**

Child's Name _____ **Ariel** _____ Date __ **10/22/06** ____ Observer _ **Ted** _____

Domain: SCIENTIFIC CONCEPTUAL UNDERSTANDINGS
Early Learning Indicator: EI #17 Uses senses to investigate characteristics and behaviors in the physical and natural worlds and begins to form explanations of observations and explorations.

Child's Progress towards the Outcome: *Circle the appropriate rating*

First Steps	**Making Progress Towards the Outcome**	**Accomplishing the Outcome**
Uses obvious sensory information to explore the world, reacting more physically than verbally.	Uses senses to explore the world (not just through the obvious), making 1 – 2 simple comments describing sensory experiences.	Uses multiple senses to explore the world and makes 1 or more detailed comments describing sensory experiences.

Check off whatever applies to the context of this observation:

☑ Child-initiated activity	☐ Done independently	☑ Time spent (1-5 mins.)
☐ Teacher-initiated activity	☑ Done with adult guidance	☐ Time spent (5-15 mins.)
☑ New task for this child	☑ Done with peer(s)	☐ More than 15 mins.
☐ Familiar task for this child		

Anecdotal Note: Describe what you saw the child do and/or heard the child say.

Today, our heater turned on for the first time. Ariel looked around and said, "What's that smell?" We all noticed that there was a musty smell coming from the heater. Ariel joined me and some other children over by the heater to smell and to feel the warm air. She giggled as she felt the warm air coming from the vents. "It tickles," she said.

DRAFT July 2006

New Mexico PreK
Focused Portfolio Collection Form

Child's Name _____**José**_____ Date __**11/12/06**__ Observer __**Marlena**__

Domain: SCIENTIFIC CONCEPTUAL UNDERSTANDINGS
Early Learning Indicator: EI #17 Uses senses to investigate characteristics and behaviors in the physical and natural worlds and begins to form explanations of observations and explorations.

Child's Progress towards the Outcome: *Circle the appropriate rating*

First Steps	**Making Progress Towards the Outcome**	**Accomplishing the Outcome**
Uses obvious sensory information to explore the world, reacting more physically than verbally.	Uses senses to explore the world (not just through the obvious), making 1 – 2 simple comments describing sensory experiences.	Uses multiple senses to explore the world and makes 1 or more detailed comments describing sensory experiences.

Check off whatever applies to the context of this observation:

☑ Child-initiated activity   ☑ Done independently   ☐ Time spent (1-5 mins.)
☐ Teacher-initiated activity   ☐ Done with adult guidance   ☐ Time spent (5-15 mins.)
☑ New task for this child   ☐ Done with peer(s)   ☑ More than 15 mins.
☐ Familiar task for this child

Anecdotal Note: Describe what you saw the child do and/or heard the child say.

Jose spent a long time with the finger paints today, mixing several colors right on the table with his hands. He made several handprints, then covered them over, and traced designs with his index finger. I helped him place a paper down over his painting so he could have a picture to take home.

©Gronlund 2006 adapted from Gronlund and Engel 2001   *DRAFT July 2006*

New Mexico PreK
Focused Portfolio Collection Form

Child's Name _____ *Marcus* _____ Date _*2/21/07*_ _____ Observer _____*Audrey*_____

Domain: SELF, FAMILY AND COMMUNITY
Early Learning Indicator: EI #21 Adapts behaviors to fit different situations (for example, accepts
transitions, follows daily routines and/or incorporates cultural
expectations).

Child's Progress towards the Outcome: *Circle the appropriate rating*

First Steps	**Making Progress Towards the Outcome**	**Accomplishing the Outcome**
Adapts behavior in one situation or adapts behavior only once in a while.	Adapts behavior in more than one situation and on a more regular basis.	Adapts behavior frequently in a variety of situations.

Check off whatever applies to the context of this observation:

☐ Child-initiated activity   ☐ Done independently   ☐ Time spent (1-5 mins.)
☒ Teacher-initiated activity   ☒ Done with adult guidance   ☐ Time spent (5-15 mins.)
☒ New task for this child   ☒ Done with peer(s)   ☐ More than 15 mins.
☐ Familiar task for this child

Anecdotal Note: Describe what you saw the child do and/or heard the child say.

Marcus got very quiet today when an elder visited the classroom to tell a tribal story. He
listened carefully and answered her questions when asked. We see this happening more
frequently with him when visitors come. He participated in the drumming activity and later,
lined up some of the children to dance as he played the drums.

©Gronlund 2006 adapted from Gronlund and Engel 2001

DRAFT July 2006

New Mexico PreK
Focused Portfolio Collection Form

Child's Name _____Alia_____ Date __10/14/06__ Observer ___Kathryn___

Domain: SELF, FAMILY AND COMMUNITY
Early Learning Indicator: EI #21 Adapts behaviors to fit different situations (for example, accepts transitions, follows daily routines and/or incorporates cultural expectations).

Child's Progress towards the Outcome: *Circle the appropriate rating*

First Steps	**Making Progress Towards the Outcome**	**Accomplishing the Outcome**
Adapts behavior in one situation or adapts behavior only once in a while.	Adapts behavior in more than one situation and on a more regular basis.	Adapts behavior frequently in a variety of situations.

Check off whatever applies to the context of this observation:

- ❑ Child-initiated activity
- ❑ Teacher-initiated activity
- ❑ New task for this child
- ☑ Familiar task for this child

- ❑ Done independently
- ❑ Done with adult guidance
- ❑ Done with peer(s)

- ❑ Time spent (1-5 mins.)
- ❑ Time spent (5-15 mins.)
- ❑ More than 15 mins.

Anecdotal Note: Describe what you saw the child do and/or heard the child say.

Alia has learned our routines at school. She helps with clean-up time almost every day without a reminder. Each day, she remembers to wash her hands before snack, and waits to pour her juice until everyone is sitting down. She anticipates going outside after story time and gets her jacket from her cubby if it's cool outdoors.

©Gronlund 2006 adapted from Gronlund and Engel 2001   *DRAFT July 2006*

**New Mexico PreK
Focused Portfolio Collection Form**

Child's Name _____**Monica**_____ Date __**3/7/07**__ Observer_____**Richard**_____

Domain: SELF, FAMILY AND COMMUNITY
Early Learning Indicator: EI #21 Adapts behaviors to fit different situations (for example, accepts transitions, follows daily routines and/or incorporates cultural expectations).

Child's Progress towards the Outcome: *Circle the appropriate rating*

First Steps	**Making Progress Towards the Outcome**	**Accomplishing the Outcome**
Adapts behavior in one situation or adapts behavior only once in a while.	Adapts behavior in more than one situation and on a more regular basis.	Adapts behavior frequently in a variety of situations.

Check off whatever applies to the context of this observation:

❏ Child-initiated activity	❏ Done independently	❏ Time spent (1-5 mins.)
☒ Teacher-initiated activity	☒ Done with adult guidance	❏ Time spent (5-15 mins.)
❏ New task for this child	❏ Done with peer(s)	❏ More than 15 mins.
☒ Familiar task for this child		

Anecdotal Note: Describe what you saw the child do and/or heard the child say.

Monica cries and covers her ears whenever the fire drill alarms sound. We try to prepare her and be near her when they are scheduled. We encourage her to talk about feeling scared and reassure her that they will stop shortly. Her reaction is not quite as strong as it was in the fall. And, when the fire drill is over, she will tell us how the firemen keep us safe.

©Gronlund 2006 adapted from Gronlund and Engel 2001

DRAFT July 2006

New Mexico PreK
Focused Portfolio Collection Form

Child's Name _____ Joseph _____ Date __11/3/07__ Observer ___Judith_____

Domain: SELF, FAMILY AND COMMUNITY
Early Learning Indicator: EI #21 Adapts behaviors to fit different situations (for example, accepts
transitions, follows daily routines and/or incorporates cultural
expectations).

Child's Progress towards the Outcome: *Circle the appropriate rating*

First Steps	**Making Progress Towards the Outcome**	**Accomplishing the Outcome**
Adapts behavior in one situation or adapts behavior only once in a while.	Adapts behavior in more than one situation and on a more regular basis.	Adapts behavior frequently in a variety of situations.

Check off whatever applies to the context of this observation:		
☑ Child-initiated activity	☑ Done independently	☐ Time spent (1-5 mins.)
☐ Teacher-initiated activity	☐ Done with adult guidance	☐ Time spent (5-15 mins.)
☑ New task for this child	☑ Done with peer(s)	☐ More than 15 mins.
☐ Familiar task for this child		

Anecdotal Note: Describe what you saw the child do and/or heard the child say.

A new boy started at our school last week. Joseph announced, "I'll be your friend, 'kay?" Then, Joseph proceeded to take the boy's hand and show him all around the room. He sat with him at circle and snack times. He talked him through clean-up time and going outside. This continued for several days. Now, the boys often play together and sit together.

©Gronlund 2006 adapted from Gronlund and Engel 2001   *DRAFT July 2006*

A Collection of Observation Notes about Claudia

Claudia, a Four-Year-Old

The observation notes that follow document Claudia's development across several areas. All of these observations occurred over a three-month period in the fall. Read through these notes about Claudia and consider the following questions as you think about Claudia and the documentation about her activities over time.

- What can and does this child do? What are the child's interests and how does he/she show them? What specific skills does the child have?
- What would the next steps be for the child in her/his development? What is the child not doing yet?
- What would you plan to do to help the child build on his/her strengths and interests and to work on what he/she is not doing yet? What materials, activities, teacher support, peer support, and special resources would you use?

Claudia's Fall Language Observation
(4 years 1 month)

Claudia announces, "I'm going to Tucson with my family—my mom and dad and my sister. And we are going to stay in a hotel with a swimming pool." She then carefully selects red, yellow, blue, and green markers and makes a rainbow. She then draws four people. She says, "Look! It's my family in a rainbow."

Claudia's Fall Problem-Solving Observation
(4 years 2 months)

It is afternoon Discovery Time after naptime. The large pattern blocks are out on a table. The children have been exploring them the past two weeks. Claudia is at the table by herself. She takes a large yellow hexagon and adds six triangles. Then she starts to layer the shapes. She plays there for some time. Then her dad arrives to take her home. "Dada, come see what I'm doing," she says. She undoes her work and redoes it exactly the way it was.

Claudia's Fall Social/Emotional Observation
(4 years 2 months)

Claudia has become more comfortable separating from her parents at drop-off time. Today she comforts Emilia, who cries after her mom leaves. Claudia says, "It's okay. Mommy's coming back." She looks at me and says, "Mommy always comes back, right, Michele?" I smile and nod yes. Claudia gently puts her arm around Emilia and says, "I miss my mom. But see, I'm not crying." At pickup time Claudia tells Emilia's mom, "Emilia was crying for you, but I told her you would come back."

Claudia's Fall Writing Sample
(4 years 1 month)

Claudia often asks for the Sleeping Beauty story tape. She often acts out the story. Today she gets lined story paper and says, "I'm writing the Sleeping Beauty story." She then draws a picture with black pen and paints it with watercolors. "This is the picture of her sleeping on the bed."

Claudia's Fall Gross Motor Observation
(4 years 2 months)

Claudia plays on the climbing equipment with Quinn and Fernando. All three of them are growling and roaring. Claudia climbs easily up the ladder to the platform. Quinn says, "Okay, I'm a baby jaguar." He paws the air in front of Claudia. She responds by saying, "Now there are two baby jaguars!" She moves quickly around the platform, jumps on the slide, and slides down. Then she runs around and climbs back up again.

You've Observed the Children:
So Now What?

When observing, an important task is to identify each child's Zone of Proximal Developments, or ZPD, which is (according to Gaye Gronlund and Marlyn James in *Focused Observations*) the "place where children do not quite have independent skills, but where they can be successful with adult or peer support. . . . When a task is within a child's ZPD, the child can become more and more independent in completing it."

Laura Berk and Adam Winsler, in *Scaffolding Children's Learning*, define the adult's role in scaffolding or supporting a child in her ZPD this way:

> According to Vygotsky, the role of education is to provide children with experiences that are in their ZPDs—activities that challenge children but can be accomplished with sensitive adult guidance. Consequently, adults carry much responsibility for making sure that children's learning is maximized by actively leading them along the developmental pathway. The teacher's role, rather than instructing children in what they are ready for or giving them tasks for which they have already acquired the necessary mental operations, is to keep tasks in children's ZPDs, or slightly above their level of independent functioning.

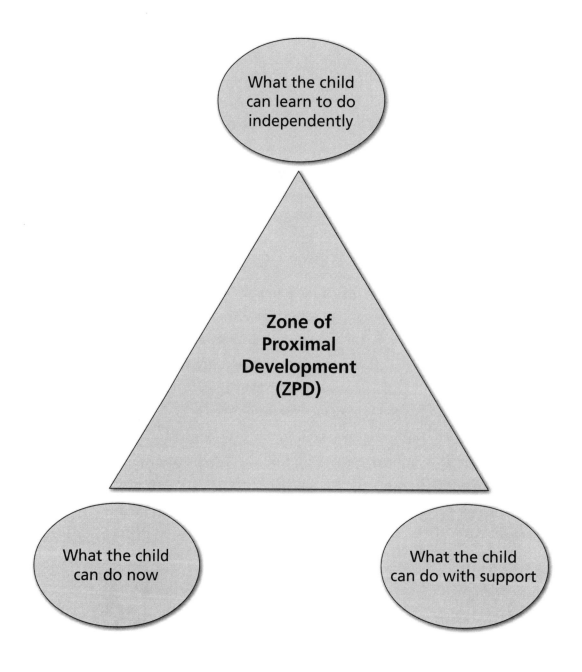

Appendix B
Case Studies and Anecdotes

Additional Case Studies

(to be used with Staff Development Activity 1 or with any other activities that you wish)

Dramatic Play (short version)

Leyonna (4 years 7 months) and Amber (4 years 10 months) are playing in the housekeeping area of the classroom. Teacher Della walks over, sits down at the table, and asks, "What are you girls doing over here?" They immediately begin bringing her cups, saying, "This is orange juice," and plates with plastic pieces of pizza on them. Della pretends to drink and eat, conversing with the girls about what kind of pizza it is and what else they can cook. The girls answer her questions and continue to repeat the same actions again and again.

Dramatic Play (long version)

Leyonna (4 years 7 months) and Amber (4 years 10 months) are playing in the housekeeping area of the classroom. Teacher Della walks over, sits down at the table, and asks, "What are you girls doing over here?" They immediately begin bringing her cups, saying, "This is orange juice," and plates with plastic pieces of pizza on them. She pretends to drink and eat, conversing with the girls about what kind of pizza it is and what else they can cook. The girls answer her questions and continue to repeat the same actions again and again. Della suggests that they may need to go to the grocery store and get some different things to cook. She wonders aloud if they need to make a grocery list. The girls respond enthusiastically and dictate items for Della to write down on a piece of paper. Della encourages them to look around at the items they have in the housekeeping area so that they can go "shopping." She then provides them with grocery bags, gives them the list, and sends them on their way. The girls stay with this activity for approximately fifteen minutes, checking in with Della even when she is working with other children across the classroom.

Farm Animal Play

Cassidy (5 years 4 months) is playing with farm animals and the silo. Noah (4 years 9 months) pushes some of the animals over and says, "These are mine." Cassidy asks him to stop, but Noah continues. Cassidy says, "Noah, I'm playing with this. Go away." Noah says, "You have too many animals and I want some." Cassidy says, "Well, wait until I'm done." Noah says, "But I don't want to" and proceeds to grab for the animals. A tug-of-war ensues.

Playdough Table

At the playdough table, comments such as "You can't come to my birthday" are being said back and forth between the three- and four-year-old children.

Sand Area

When the children go outside they notice that the sand area is full of leaves from the storm the previous night. They run to the teacher and ask her to get the leaves out of the sand so they can make roads for their trucks. They tell her that the leaves are in their way and ask her why they are in the sand.

Rescue

Two boys, ages four and five, are playing rescue, running around the play yard and taking "injured" children to the top of the climber, which they are using as a hospital. They tell the other children that they cannot climb up to the top because it is a hospital and it is too dangerous.

Anecdotes to Analyze for Staff Development Activity 18

(or for any other activities that you wish)

Cassidy (4 years 7 months)

Cassidy and another child are playing a game in the housekeeping area. Cassidy is the mom holding the baby, while the other child is sitting at the table pretending to sign out the baby to Cassidy. Cassidy says, "Now it's my turn." They switch places. The other child says, "Can you get the baby for me?" Cassidy replies, "She's in the other classroom." The other child asks, "Which class do I go to?" Cassidy says, "Go down to your right," and proceeds to draw a map. Both girls say "Bye-bye."

Cassidy takes the baby and says, "She's big. She's really heavy." They both walk to the library and get the *Night Noises* book (which was read to them earlier). They sit on the couch and "read" the story to the baby.

Gabriel (4 years 10 months)

When sitting at snack, Gabriel notices that he doesn't have a napkin. The teacher tells him that there is one for everyone. He begins to count each child and looks to see if each has a napkin. He counts all 15 children and 15 napkins.

Josiah (3 years 11 months)

While adding color to a water-and-oil experiment, Josiah shakes his glass. The color starts to mix with the oil and water. Josiah says, "It has tiny bubbles all over and it's turning blue." He then says, "The bubbles are floating back to the top of the jar and going back down when I shake it."

Kristen (4 years 9 months)

Kristen is working in the art area. After 10 minutes, she gets up from her chair and walks over to her cubby. She gets out a coloring book, walks over to Casey, and asks, "Can I use my coloring book?" Casey tells Kristen she can, but only if she shares with the other children. Kristen says, "Yes, I can share my coloring book, but I have to tear out the pages myself." Casey says, "Okay, Kristen."

Jackie (3 years 10 months)

Jackie is playing at the playdough table and says, "Look, I made a birthday cake. Tomorrow is my birthday and I need to bake my cake. Where is the oven for cakes?" She walks over to the art area and gets a box and says, "This is the oven. Be careful, it's hot."

Jake (3 years 3 months)

Jack is running around the classroom with a plastic dinosaur in his hand telling the other children that he is a T. Rex. "Grrrr. I'm a T. Rex! Grrrr." The teacher suggests that he build a special place in the blocks for his dinosaur so that he won't scare the other children. He goes into the block area and puts four blocks around the dinosaur, then gets up and runs around the room again.

Marc (3 years 6 months), Ariel (4 years 3 months)

Marc and Ariel are playing in the family life area. Marc is the kitty and Ariel is getting him a saucer of milk. She makes a bed for him with blankets and pillows and tells him it is time to go to bed. Marc goes over to the pile of blankets and pillows and lies down. Ariel covers him with another blanket and says, "Night-night, kitty. See you in the morning." She tiptoes to a chair and sits down.

Appendix C
Video Vignettes

To prepare for staff development activities, we suggest that you copy the PowerPoint file from the CD-ROM to your computer. Then, when you are ready to lead a group of teachers in an activity that uses a video vignette, you can show the PowerPoint slides using the file you saved to your computer and then insert the DVD into your disc drive to show the vignettes.

To go with Staff Development Activity 7:
Vignette 1, "Tubes and Bottles"

To go with Staff Development Activity 14:
Vignette 2, "Washing Hands and Snack"

To go with Staff Development Activity 17:
Vignette 3, "Painting"

To go with Staff Development Activity 19:
Vignette 4, "Three Young Writers"

To go with Staff Development Activity 22:
Vignette 5, "Working with a Puzzle"

To go with Staff Development Activity 23:
Vignette 6, "Making Music"
Vignette 7, "Listening to a Story"
Vignette 8, "Playdough, Cups, and Binoculars"

Appendix D
List of PowerPoint Slides

The PowerPoint slides on the accompanying CD are keyed to the following Staff Development Activities in chapters 4–7:

Activity 1.   Identifying Teaching Strategies, slides 1–5

Activity 2.   Engaging Children in Learning, slide 6

Activity 3.   Breathing Out and Breathing In, slides 7–9

Activity 4.   When to Sustain and When to Interrupt, slides 10–12

Activity 5.   Identifying Early Learning Standards in Self-Initiated Play, slides 13–14

Activity 6.   Analyzing Early Learning Standards and Generating Curricular Ideas, slide 15

Activity 7.   Observation Practice: Encouraging and Extending a Child's Interests in an Intentional Curricular Activity, slide 16

Activity 8.   Identifying Early Learning Standards for Classroom Learning Areas, slides 17–18

Activity 9.   Webbing Daily Routines and Early Learning Standards, slides 19–21

Activity 10. Using Planning and Reflection Frameworks, slides 22–23

Activity 11. Analyzing Lesson Plans, slides 24–25

Activity 12. Projects, Studies, and Standards, slides 26–27

Activity 13. Using Observation and Documentation in Administering Developmental Screening Instruments, slides 28–29

Activity 14. Observing a Child at Snack Time, slides 30–31

Activity 15. Factual vs. Interpretive Documentation, slides 32–35

Activity 16. Interpreting Children's Actions, slides 36–37

Activity 17. Using Summative Anecdotes, slides 38–39

Activity 18. Identifying Developmental Areas and Specific Skills, slides 40–41

Activity 19. Identifying Steps of Progress, slides 42–43

Activity 20. Quick and Easy or In-Depth Documentation? slides 44–45

Activity 21. Rating Children's Performance by Reviewing Portfolio Documentation, slides 46–47

Activity 22. A Focused Observation on Problem Solving, slides 48–49

Activity 23. Building a Case about a Child across Domains, slides 50–52

Activity 24. You've Observed the Children: So Now What? slides 53–56

Appendix E
Making the Case for Play Policy: Research-Based Reasons to Support Play-Based Environments

by Dolores A. Stegelin

Play is a child's life and the means by which he comes to understand the world he lives in.

> —SUSAN ISAACS
> SOCIAL DEVELOPMENT IN YOUNG CHILDREN

"Making the Case for Play Policy: Research-Based Reasons to Support Play-Based Environments," by Dolores A. Stegelin, was first published in *Young Children* 60, no. 2 (2005):76–85. © 2005 by NAEYC. Reprinted with permission from the National Association for the Education of Young Children. www.naeyc.org.

Contemporary early childhood classrooms are complex places where the opportunities for play are few. The need for effective play policy has never been greater. We early childhood professionals know that physically and mentally engaging, play-based activity is essential for overall healthy child development. But these days we often find ourselves defending play-based curriculum and instructional approaches to families, administrators, even colleagues.

This article can help teachers and directors become eloquent and effective advocates of play-based early learning environments. It defines play and play policy and discusses distinct research areas that support play policy and practice for physical, cognitive, social, and emotional development within diverse early childhood settings. Also presented are three anecdotal examples of current challenges to play-based curriculum. I hope the information serves as a useful tool for developing strategies for organizing a play policy effort.

Defining Play and Play Policy

Play research has many important dimensions, and play policy is an untapped and fertile area for research (Stegelin 2002b). An appropriate definition of play is necessary for effective play policy development and implementation. Definitions of play emerge from three perspectives: (1) the exploratory and open-ended nature of play; (2) the intrinsic, evolutionary, and synergistic nature of play; and (3) the developmental aspects of play (Anderson 1998).

The *exploratory nature* of play has been studied extensively (Pellegrini & Perlmutter 1989; O'Neill-Wagner, Bolig, & Price 1994; Bolig et al. 1998) and is captured in this definition: "Play is an essential part of every child's life and vital to their development. It is the way children explore the world around them and develop and practise skills. It is essential for physical, emotional and spiritual growth, for intellectual and educational development, and for acquiring social and behavioural skills" (Hampshire Play Policy Forum 2002, 1). Play and exploration behaviors are characteristic behaviors of both young humans and primates and are observable in a variety of contexts that include specific conditions, such as availability of toys and objects for manipulation and freedom from excessive anxiety. Play behaviors are often preceded by exploration, so it is important that the environment encourages exploration.

Using Manipulatives and Other Play-Based Approaches in First Grade

- -

Mrs. Alvarez is an experienced primary teacher in a large public school system. She has twice been named Teacher of the Year at the elementary school and is now working toward a master's degree in elementary education.

Today, during unit meetings, three other first grade teachers want to know why Mrs. Alvarez does not use the rigorous math and science curriculum recommended by the school district. The new curriculum is heavily teacher-directed, uses daily worksheets and drills, and requires standardized testing every nine weeks.

Mrs. Alvarez says, "You know, I really thought about making a change this year. The new textbooks are attractive, and in some ways the curriculum seems easier in terms of planning and teaching. But then I thought about how much my students really look forward to math and science and how well they have done the past several years on the school district's end-of-the-year tests. I decided that even though it takes more time and resources, I really believe in a hands-on approach to learning.

"Besides," she adds, "six-year-olds need time and space to explore, suggest activities, make up their own hypotheses, and feel their ideas really do count. My math and science activities require the children to think, work together, and record their own answers. I like the opportunities for creative thinking, for students to think for themselves and to move around and take charge of their time. For now, I'm going to keep using manipulatives.

"And yes," she says, "I know my classroom is louder and messier than most of yours, but so far the parents agree with my approach. I'm convinced that six-year-olds learn best with interactive, cooperative learning experiences."

The *evolutionary and intrinsic* nature of play is reflected in the creative aspect of play that is open-ended, unpredictable, unique, and "comedic" or imbued with "surprise" (Salthe 1991). From the child's perspective, the opportunity to play is an invitation that turns into a "self-fueled, synergistic, inherently rewarding, but not necessarily rewarded process called play" (Anderson 1998, 103). The resulting patterns of play activity lead to a summative experience known as "fun" (Anderson 1998). Thus, a definition of play should include the *intrinsic, evolutionary, synergistic,* and *motivating* aspects of play.

The *developmental* aspects of play include the more predictable structures of play associated with children's social, cognitive, language, physical, and creative development from infancy through the primary years. At every stage of development, play activity takes on some degree of predictability but still allows for spontaneous, fluid, repetitive, and turn-taking behaviors. The responsibility of the early childhood professional and the policy advocate is to provide appropriate contexts in which these predictable and developmental behaviors can occur, as delineated in the Hampshire play policy statement (2002) above.

In summary, play policy advocates can use the following essential features to define play:

- Play requires specific *conditions of safety and psychological security* that are essential for the child to engage in relaxed, open-ended, and exploratory behaviors.
- Play includes *exploratory behaviors* that involve manipulation of objects, toys, and other materials, and this exploratory nature of play often precedes actual focused play behavior.
- Play is an important *evolutionary behavior* that is essential for healthy development to occur across all areas: social, cognitive, language, physical, and creative.
- Play is behavior that *sustains the healthy development of the individual* and the larger sociocultural fabric of society and reflects the contexts in which the child lives (home, community, and the larger society).

Linking Play to Play Policy

Many contemporary play policy initiatives have originated in the United Kingdom, while systematic play research has been done in the United States and other parts of the world. Effective play policy is founded on clear articulation of what is meant by play and a commitment to respond to children's needs and wishes (PLAYLINK 2001). But what is a play policy? According to Play Wales (2002), a play policy is a statement of both an organization's current play provision and its aspirations for change and development. Play policy usually includes the following important criteria (PLAYLINK 2001; Play Wales 2002):

- the objectives of play and play-related services and activities;
- the connection between acceptable levels of risk and healthy play;

- an assumption of inclusive play settings for all children (ethnic and developmental diversity);
- the criteria for evaluating a quality play environment;
- the essential and inherent aspect of play as part of a child's cultural life; and
- the need to create and integrate play opportunities in the general environment.

Developing and implementing effective play policy takes time, commitment, and perseverance. Effective play policy at the local, state, national, and international levels evolves over time and is the result of many attempts. The primary aim of play policy is to

- articulate and promote the importance of play for all children,
- recognize that all children have the right to play, as stated in the 1989 United Nations Convention on the Rights of the Child, and
- enable all children to have equal access to good quality play environments in their local communities. (Hampshire Play Policy Forum 2002)

Early childhood professionals involved in play policy development can use the above definitions of play and play policy to bolster their play policy rationales and to strengthen their role as advocates. Essential to policy development is the use of research-based information for integrating systematic play into child care, Head Start, preschool, and K–3 settings. Three critical research areas support the rationale for play-based environments.

Research Focus 1: Active Play and Health-Related Indicators

The first area of research that addresses the critical need for play-based learning environments—especially physically active and vigorous play—is health related. The rapidly increasing rates of childhood obesity and weight-related health problems are exacerbated by physical inactivity and sedentary routines. Experts point to the prevalence of junk food marketed to children, too much television and other sedentary entertainment, and fewer families sitting down together to eat (American Heart Association 2005).

In addition, mental health research points out the link between physical exercise and the reduced incidence of anxiety, depression, and behavioral problems in young children (U.S. Department of Health and Human Services 1996). Physical activity through play alleviates stress and helps children learn to manage feelings and gain a sense of self-control (Aronson 2002; Sanders 2002). Therefore, integrated and physically demanding play requires the use of both mind and body (Larkin 2002).

The Link between Physical Inactivity and Health Problems

Rates of childhood obesity in the United States and England have doubled since 1970 (Edmunds, Waters, & Elliott 2001; Elliott 2002). Even some infants and toddlers are being diagnosed as obese by their second or third birthdays. According to the American Heart Association (2005) the U.S. obesity epidemic is now affecting the youngest children, with more than 10 percent of two- to five-year-olds overweight—up from 7 percent in 1994. Childhood obesity is related to five critical health and psychosocial problems: (1) high blood pressure, (2) type 2 diabetes, (3) coronary heart disease, (4) social rejection, and (5) school failure and dropout (Freedman et al. 2001).

Early childhood professionals and play advocates can bolster the case for physically active and play-based environments by citing current information from national and international entities. For example, in the United States, the Centers for Disease Control and Prevention (CDC) assumes a preventive health stance, advocating for greater physical activity, balanced nutrition, and much more active lifestyles. Because 25 percent of American children are obese and 61 percent of adults are overweight (Guo et al. 2002), it is difficult to overstate the dimensions of the problem. The CDC uses the Body Mass Index (BMI) with children as a predictor of adult obesity (Guo et al. 2002). Advocates for physically active play environments can use these facts to emphasize the seriousness of health issues for children in sedentary care and learning environments and stress the need for all types of play, both indoor and outdoor.

The Health Benefits of Physically Active Play

Daily schedules, play objects, and adult-child interactions can be contrasted in high- and low-quality early childhood settings to make advocacy points. For example, high-quality early childhood classrooms incorporate (1) daily schedules that routinely include active indoor and rough-and-tumble outdoor play (Rivkin 2000); (2) kinesthetic movement as part of concept learning; (3) integration of music, movement, and creative expression; and (4) adult-child interactions that model moderate to high levels of physical activity. In contrast, low-quality settings (1) do not have predictable schedules for indoor and outdoor play; (2) employ more passive and sedentary learning strategies such as television viewing or adult-directed teaching; (3) minimize opportunities for kinesthetic movement and learning; and (4) do not encourage creative expression through physical exercise, dance, and movement.

At the elementary school level, organized sports and physical education also provide play opportunities. Supporters of sports as a form of play suggest that sports contain many of the elements used to describe play (Frost, Wortham, & Reifel 2001). The policy issue of regular and scheduled outdoor recess in public schools is being studied, but research indicates that children need recess for a variety of reasons, including socialization opportunities, respite from attention to classroom tasks, a break that allows them to give maximum attention to their work once again, and the obvious benefits of physical activity to counter sedentary lifestyles and patterns of obesity (Pelligrini & Bjorklund 1996; Jarrett 2002).

In summary, play advocates can state the following health benefits of active play to bolster their play advocacy efforts:

- large muscle development through reaching, grasping, crawling, running, climbing, skipping, and balancing;
- fine motor skill development and eye-hand coordination as the child handles objects in play;
- increased metabolism and energy consumption through routine physical activity;
- decreased weight and heart-related problems;
- reduced levels of chronic stress; and
- increased feelings of success, self-control, and social competence. (Piaget 1962; Piaget & Inhelder 1969)

This research area may represent the most urgent rationale for physically active and rigorous play for all children. Teachers, parents, and administrators should place health concerns high on their priority list when developing play policy. What can be more important than the overall health of young children?

Research Focus 2: Brain Research—The Critical Link between Play and Optimal Cognitive and Physical Development

Brain research now documents observable differences in the quantity and quality of brain cell development between young children with stimulating and nonstimulating early learning experiences during the first 36 months of life. Children's play behaviors become more complex and abstract as they progress through childhood (Piaget 1962; Johnson, Christie, & Yawkey 1987). In very concrete terms, the recent flurry of research related to brain growth and development clearly supports and undergirds the necessity of active, physical, and cognitively stimulating play for *all* young children (Zwillich 2001).

Information gathered through new brain-imaging techniques is already playing a major role in how public policy decisions are made. Cognitive skills advance during problem solving with play materials, ideas, events, and people. This begins in infancy—for example, when a baby makes the startling discovery that shaking a rattle causes a sound reaction. Stimulating play environments facilitate progress to higher levels of thought throughout childhood. Functional magnetic resonance imaging (fMRI), positron emission tomography (PET), and other brain-scanning tools are for the first time providing meaningful insights into the way human brains change and develop during the early years of life (Zwillich 2001).

Neuroscientists point out that the connections between brain cells that underlie new learning become hard-wired if they are used repeatedly but can be diminished if they are not (Morrison 2004). However, caution is warranted here: we should not interpret brain research findings to label or place limits on children whose brains do not appear to be "normal" at very young ages. What is clear among the varied brain research findings is that younger children need (1) physical activity, (2) hands-on activities that develop large and fine motor skills, (3) opportunities for eye-hand coordination activities, (4) auditory and visually stimulating environments, and (5) consistent daily routines that actively engage the child both in the home and preschool environments.

Defending Learning Centers to the Assistant Principal

- -

Mr. Hemminger, a first-year kindergarten teacher, graduated top of his class with a bachelor's degree in early childhood education. He impresses everyone with his enthusiasm, eagerness to learn about new teaching approaches, and obvious delight in working with five-year-olds.

Mr. Hemminger advocates and models a highly interactive, hands-on approach to learning, and his classroom is known for creative expression, high levels of family involvement, and a learning environment that invites everyone to come in, observe, and participate. The classroom includes five learning centers, small-group cooperative-learning opportunities, and a high level of child-initiated planning and assessment of learning experiences.

Mr. Hemminger is guided by state and local school curriculum guidelines, content expectations, and assessment procedures. He uses many different assessment strategies, including observation, work sampling, portfolios, and periodic testing.

During Mr. Hemminger's first evaluation, the assistant principal asks about his use of center-based learning. "Isn't that for preschool children? There have been some complaints by other teachers about the noise level in this classroom. Is there some way you can tone it down a bit? Shouldn't the children be doing more seat work, silent reading, and worksheets? After all, they'll soon be taking a standardized test."

Mr. Hemminger explains that he has specific learning objectives and outcomes in mind for all daily activities. He points out that research supports active, exploratory learning at the kindergarten level. He is so confident in his center-based approach to teaching that he says he is not concerned about testing outcomes in the spring. "The children are learning *and* they are having fun. I believe that if they are involved in the planning of the day's activities, have a chance to create hypotheses and then explore them, and have daily interactions with their peers, they will learn much more than they would in isolation or in completing seat work."

"Well, we'll see how it goes this year," says the assistant principal. "I'll be noting the noise level and the way your children perform in April."

Research Focus 3: The Link between Play, Early Literacy, and Social Competence

Research on play and its relationship to social and language development has been conducted for many years (for example, Parten 1932). Current research on early literacy outcomes shows a relationship between active, socially engaging play and early language and literacy development (Neuman & Roskos 1993; Owocki 1999; Morrow 2001). Social skills also grow through play experiences as the child moves from enjoying simple contact with another person to learning to cooperate, take turns, and play by the rules. Social skills, oral language development, and dramatic play go hand in hand. Children who are provided play opportunities in same-age and multi-age settings broaden their own understandings of the social world and of language diversity (Roskos et al. 1995).

Relationships between Social Play, Language, and Early Literacy Development

The growing emphasis on the teaching of early literacy skills in child care, Head Start, and other early learning settings stems from this important research linkage (Neuman & Roskos 1993). Play policy advocates can find much support in the research literature for social play as a significant contributor to early language development and later literacy indicators (Strickland & Strickland 1997; Christie 1998; Owocki 1999; Morrow 2001; International Reading Association 2002). A noted group of early literacy specialists (Neuman & Roskos 1993; Goldhaber et al. 1996; Morrow 1997; Strickland & Strickland 1997; Christie 1998; Morrow 2001) are documenting the significant effect of hands-on, socially engaging early literacy experiences on the literacy readiness and prereading skills of young children in preschool and kindergarten settings. Although not always regarded as "reading" in a formal sense, acquisition of these print-meaning associations is viewed as an important precursor to more skilled reading (Mason 1980; Goodman 1986).

Play advocates can argue for a "materials intervention" strategy that involves making play areas resemble the literacy environments that children encounter at home and in their communities (Christie 1998). Since not all families offer equal opportunities for young children to engage in rich literacy events, it is especially important that child care and other early learning settings provide these play-based experiences for equal access to literacy building skills. And children are more likely to engage in play-related reading and writing activities if available materials invite these types of activities (Morrow & Rand 1991; Vukelich 1991; Christie & Enz 1992).

Research shows that the following play-based activities in the early childhood setting promote social awareness and early literacy development:

- *Use of literacy props*—puppets, stuffed animals, dramatic-play items, books, markers, signs, paper of many types—along with adult modeling and encouragement, fosters greater print awareness, verbal expression, and social interactions (Christie & Enz 1992; Neuman & Roskos 1992; Goldhaber et al. 1996). Literacy props, especially developmentally appropriate books and writing tools, placed in learning centers *beyond* the traditional reading and meeting areas (such as block, puzzle and manipulative, dramatic play, and natural science) increase both the quality and quantity of early literacy play-based experiences (Goldhaber et al. 1996; Neuman & Roskos 1993). One study (Neuman & Roskos 1993) found a significant increase in book handling, reading, and writing choices by children (98% African-American and 2% Hispanic) after Head Start teachers set up and participated in a play "office" setting.

- *Integration of art activities* (such as painting, finger painting, and drawing) in the curriculum promotes writing and print awareness (Morrow 2001). Play in the visual arts is immediate and responsive rather than planned out and goal-directed (Johnson 1998); children learn to "invent" their own words, represent letters of the alphabet, and otherwise re-create their imaginary world through forms of printing and drawing.

- *Emphasis on environmental print* (such as labeling of blocks, learning centers, and materials within centers), along with print-rich learning environments (which include maps, newspapers, magazines, many types of books, and posters) encourages alphabet awareness, understanding that print has meaning, and the assimilation of new words in children's vocabularies (Morrow 2001).

- *Incorporation of poetry, songs, chants, storytelling, and sharing of big books* on a daily basis encourages children to verbalize their feelings, learn letter sounds (phonemic awareness) and words, and begin to understand written language through repetition with adults and peers. This is especially important for preschoolers who may have limited exposure to oral language, rituals, and storytelling at home (Morrow 2001; Stegelin 2002a).

- *Teachers should provide adequate time for children to play* and should be sensitive to matching authentic play-based literacy materials to the cultural and developmental characteristics of the children (Neuman & Roskos 1991; Christie & Wardle 1992).

In short, play policy advocates can find an abundance of current research on the positive effects of play-based early literacy experiences that increase the likelihood of positive outcomes in language and literacy development.

Explaining a Literacy Approach to a Family

Ms. Ruhnquist is a veteran child care director of a large for-profit pre-school center that provides comprehensive services for more than 100 children. Ms. Ruhnquist has a master's degree in educational administration and a bachelor's in child development. Well-organized and attentive to detail, she is respected for her understanding of early childhood development, her engaging style of family and staff interactions, and her business skills.

Today, as she enrolls four-year-old Mariah, the parents ask her about the center's approach to "teaching reading." Somewhat surprised, she listens attentively and then asks what their main concern is.

"Well, we want Mariah to know the alphabet and be able to read when she starts kindergarten. We want her to be ahead of the others and ready for higher academic work. Do you use a recognized reading curriculum?"

Ms. Ruhnquist explains that the center uses a nationally recognized early childhood curriculum that focuses on all aspects of a child's development, including language development.

"We use a play-based, child-directed approach that focuses on developing autonomy and self-reliance," she says. "In terms of language development, we have a literacy center, lots of books, and we encourage the exploration of reading and writing in six different learning centers. We focus on storytelling, exploration of different kinds of books and literature, and on phonemic awareness. But we do not teach reading per se. We believe that helping Mariah learn to love books and gain confidence in her own abilities will help her be ready for the early reading experiences in kindergarten. If you'd like to observe the classroom and talk to Mariah's teacher, you're welcome to do so before finalizing her enrollment."

The parents observe the classroom and complete Mariah's enrollment but make it clear they will be watching her progress in prereading skills.

Research Linking Play to Social Competence

Much research-based evidence supports the common-sense notion that play with others is necessary for the development of social competence, and that it in turn has a direct relationship to success in school. In fact, a convincing body of evidence has accumulated to indicate that unless children achieve minimal social competence by about age six, they have a higher probability of being at risk in adolescent and adult development (McClellan & Katz 2001). Other studies (Hartup & Moore 1990; Ladd & Profilet 1996) suggest that a child's long-term social and emotional adaptation, academic and cognitive development, and citizenship are enhanced by frequent childhood opportunities to strengthen social competence.

Early childhood educators and play advocates alike should be able to articulate this critical relationship. In addition, we can cite specific studies that document important social outcomes. For example, in the area of pretend play, research (Piaget 1962; Fein 1981; Smilansky 1990; Nourot 1998) reveals that pretend and dramatic play strengthens the child's understanding of the real world and provides opportunities for imagination to develop. Sociodramatic play provides the matrix for understanding and representing the perspectives of others and for opportunities to compromise and to stand firm in one's beliefs and intentions (Nourot 1998).

Fabes and colleagues (2003) studied the role that young children's same-sex peer interactions play in influencing early school competence. In observing 98 young children (median age of 54.77 months), they found that patterns differed for boys and girls related to school outcomes and specific play interactions. This study invites follow-up research to determine more specific gender-related differences in play. Further, these studies show that informal interactions with peers in play situations foster the social competence behaviors necessary for learning and development.

Summary

All of us can become play advocates who influence play policy in varied settings such as child care, Head Start, and public school kindergarten and primary classrooms. Early childhood professionals wanting to become more active in play policy development can point to research-based evidence that active play leads to optimal outcomes for young children. There are clear positive outcomes in the following areas:

1. *Physical and mental health indicators* reflect a direct correlation between rigorous, physically active play and reduced levels of obesity, heart-related problems, and chronic stress.

2. *Cognitive development* is optimized through active, exploratory play, as evidenced through brain scans and research

that document that active, stimulating play on a regular basis promotes optimal brain development in young children.

3. *Language and early literacy development* is enhanced through print-rich learning environments that engage children in active, reciprocal, and systematic interaction with their peers and supportive adults through books, writing experiences, manipulatives, and story-sharing routines.

4. *Social competence,* largely developed by age six, is best nurtured in young children through sociodramatic and pretend play with peers, social interactions in small group settings, and assimilation of routines and reciprocal engagement with peers and caring adults.

We make a strong case for the importance of play in early childhood education when we are able to cite research that strongly supports play and play-based environments. Play-based instructional strategies and environments are a widely discussed topic in the field these days. Many forces counter the play movement, promoting accelerated academic requirements at earlier ages, standardized testing, and accountability mandates, while also citing scheduling issues in elementary schools and safety factors. We early childhood professionals must be prepared to assume an advocacy role in the area of play policy. Parents, teachers, and administrators must be willing to speak up and speak out on behalf of the play needs of our children.

References

American Heart Association. 2005. Heart disease and stroke statistics—2005 update. Dallas, Tex.: Author. Online: www.americanheart.org/downloadable/heart/1103829139928HDSStats2005Update.pdf.

Anderson, M. 1998. The meaning of play as a human experience. In Play from birth to twelve and beyond, eds. D. Fromberg & D. Bergen, 103–08. New York: Garland.

Aronson, S. S., ed., comp. with P. Spahr. 2002. Healthy young children: A manual for programs. 4th ed. Washington, D.C.: NAEYC.

Bolig, R., C. S. Price, P. L. O'Neill-Wagner, & S. J. Suomi. 1998. Reactivity and play and exploration behaviors of young Rhesus monkeys. In Play and culture studies, Vol. 1, ed. S. Reifel, 165–77. Greenwich, Conn.: Ablex.

Christie, J., & F. Wardle. 1992. How much time is needed for play? Young Children 47 (3): 28–32.

Christie, J. F. 1998. Play as a medium for literacy development. In Play from birth to twelve and beyond, eds. D. Fromberg & D. Bergen, 50–55. New York: Garland.

Christie, J. F., & B. Enz. 1992. The effects of literacy play interventions on preschoolers' play patterns and literacy development. Early Education and Development 3: 205–20.

Edmunds, L., E. Waters, & E. Elliott. 2001. Evidence-based management of childhood obesity: Evidence-based pediatrics. British Medical Journal 323 (7318): 916–19.

Elliott, V. 2002. Adult options for childhood obesity? Doctors say the high number of extremely overweight young people is serious enough to consider radical interventions. American Medical News 45 (20): 27.

Fabes, R. A., C. L. Martin, L. D. Hanish, M. C. Anders, & D. A. Madden-Derdich. 2003. Early school competence: The roles of sex-segregated play and effortful control. Developmental Psychology 39 (5): 848–59.

Fein, G. G. 1981. Pretend play in childhood: An integrative review. Child Development 52: 1095–1118.

Freedman, D., L. Khan, W. Dietz, S. Srivinasian, & G. S. Berenson. 2001. Relationship of childhood obesity to coronary heart disease risk factors in adulthood. Pediatric 108 (3): 712.

Frost, J. L., S. C. Wortham, & S. Reifel. 2001. Play and child development. Columbus, Ohio: Merrill/Prentice-Hall.

Goldhaber, J., M. Lipson, S. Sortino, & P. Daniels. 1996. Books in the sand box? Markers in the blocks? Expanding the child's world of literacy. Childhood Education 73 (2): 88–92.

Goodman, Y. 1986. Children coming to know literacy. In Emergent literacy, eds. W. Teale & E. Sulzby, 1–14. Norwood, N.J.: Ablex.

Guo, S. S., W. Wu, W. C. Chulea, & A. F. Roche. 2002. Predicting overweight and obesity in adulthood from body mass index volume in childhood and adolescence. Journal of Clinical Nutrition 76 (3): 653–56.

Hampshire Play Policy Forum. 2002. Hampshire play policy position statement. Online: www.hants.gov.uk/childcare/playpolicy.html.

Hartup, W. W., & S. G. Moore. 1990. Early peer relations: Developmental significance and prognostic implications. Early Childhood Research Quarterly 5 (1): 1–18.

International Reading Association. 2002. What is evidence-based reading instruction? Reading standards statement. Online: www. reading.org/advocacy/standards.

Jarrett, O. S. 2002. Recess in elementary school: What does the research say? ERIC Digest EDO-PS-02-5.

Johnson, H. A. 1998. Play in the visual arts: One photographer's way-of-working. In Play from birth to twelve and beyond, eds. D. Fromberg & D. Bergen, 435–41. New York: Garland.

Johnson, J., J. Christie, & T. Yawkey. 1987. Play and early childhood development. Glenview, Ill.: Scott, Foresman.

Ladd, G. W., & S. M. Profilet. 1996. The Child Behavior Scale: A teacher-report measure of young children's aggressive, withdrawn, and prosocial behaviors. Developmental Psychology 32 (6): 1008–24.

Larkin, M. 2002. Defusing the "time bomb" of childhood obesity. The Lancet 359: (9310): 987.

Mason, J. 1980. When do children begin to read?: An exploration of four-year-old children's word reading competencies. Reading Research Quarterly 15: 203–27.

McClellan, D. E., & L. G. Katz. 2001. Assessing young children's social competence. ERIC Digest EDO-PS-01-2.

Morrison, G. M. 2004. Early childhood education today. 9th ed. Columbus, Ohio: Merrill/Prentice-Hall.

Morrow, L. M. 1997. The literacy center. York, Maine: Stenhouse.

Morrow, L. M. 2001. Literacy development in the early years. 4th ed. Boston: Allyn & Bacon.

Morrow, L. M., & M. K. Rand. 1991. Preparing the classroom environment to promote literacy during play. In Play and early literacy development, ed. J. F. Christie, 141–65. Albany: State University of New York.

Neuman, S. B., & K. Roskos. 1991. Peers as literacy informants: A description of young children's literacy conversations in play. Early Childhood Research Quarterly 6: 233–48.

Neuman, S. B., & K. Roskos. 1992. Literacy objects as cultural tools: Effects on children's literacy behaviors in play. Reading Research Quarterly 27: 202–25.

Neuman, S., & K. Roskos. 1993. Access to print for children of poverty: Differential effects of adult mediation and literacy-enriched play settings on environmental and functional print tasks. American Educational Research Journal 30 (1): 95–122.

Nourot, P. M. 1998. Sociodramatic play—Pretending together. In Play from birth to twelve and beyond, eds. D. Fromberg & D. Bergen, 378–91. New York: Garland.

O'Neill-Wagner, P. L., R. Bolig, & C. S. Price. 1994. Do play activity levels tell us something of psychosocial welfare in captive monkey groups? Communication and Cognition 27: 261–72.

Owocki, G. 1999. Literacy through play. Portsmouth, N.H.: Heinemann.

Parten, M. 1932. Social participation among preschool children. Journal of Abnormal and Social Psychology 27: 243–69.

Pelligrini, A. D., & D. F. Bjorklund. 1996. The place of recess in school: Issues in the role of recess in children's education and development. Journal of Research in Childhood Education 11: 5–13.

Pelligrini, A., & M. Perlmutter. 1989. Classroom contextual effects of children's play. Child Development 25: 289–96.

Piaget, J. 1962. Play, dreams, and imitation in childhood. New York: Norton.

Piaget, J., & B. Inhelder. 1969. The psychology of the child. New York: Basic.

PLAYLINK. 2001. Articulating play policy. London, UK: Author.

Play Wales. 2002. Defining play policy. Cardiff, UK: Author.

Rivkin, M. S. 2000. Outdoor experiences for young children. ERIC Digest EDO-RC-007.

Roskos, K., J. Vukelich, B. Christie, B. Enz, & S. Neuman. 1995. Linking literacy and play. Newark, Del.: International Reading Association.

Salthe, S. N. 1991. Development and evolution: Complexity and change in biological systems. Cambridge, Mass.: MIT Press.

Sanders, S. W. 2002. Active for life: Developmentally appropriate movement programs for young children. Washington, D.C.: NAEYC.

Smilansky, S. 1990. Sociodramatic play: Its relevance to behavior and achievement in school. In Children's play and learning: Perspectives and policy implications, eds. E. Klugman & S. Smilansky, 18–42. New York: Teachers College Press.

Stegelin, D.A. 2002a. Early literacy education: First steps toward dropout prevention. Clemson, S.C.: National Dropout Prevention Center, Clemson University.

Stegelin, D. A. 2002b. Play policy: A survey of online and professional literature. Unpublished paper presented to the Play, Policy, and Practice Forum, NAEYC Annual Conference, Nov. 20–23, New York, N.Y.

Strickland, D., & M. Strickland. 1997. Language and literacy: The poetry connection. Language Arts 74 (3): 201–05.

U.S. Department of Health and Human Services. 1996. Physical activity and health: A report of the Surgeon General. Atlanta, Ga.: Author, Centers for Disease Control and Prevention.

Vukelich, C. 1991. Learning about the functions of writing: The effects of three play settings on children's interventions and development of knowledge about writing. Unpublished paper presented at the National Reading Conference, December, Palm Springs, Calif.

Zwillich, T. 2001. Brain scan technology poised to play policy. Online: www .loni.ucla.edu/~thompson/MEDIA/RH/rh.html.